Eighth Edition

The State
of
Church Giving
through 1996

John L. Ronsvalle

Sylvia Ronsvalle

empty tomb, inc.
Champaign, Illinois
http://www.emptytomb.org

The State of Church Giving through 1996 by John and Sylvia Ronsvalle
published by empty tomb, inc.
First printing, December 1998

empty tomb, inc.
301 North Fourth Street
P.O. Box 2404
Champaign, Illinois 61825-2404
Phone: (217) 356-9519
Fax: (217) 356-2344

ISBN 0-9639962-8-2
ISSN 1097-3192

Contents _____

Tables and Figures v

Preface ix

Summary 1

Introduction 3

1. Church Member Giving, 1968-1996 7

2. Church Member Giving for 44 Denominations, 1995 to 1996 21

3. Church Member Giving in Denominations Defined by
   Organizational Affiliation, 1968, 1985, and 1996 25

4. Church Member Giving for Eleven Denominations, 1921-1996 37

5. Church Member Giving and Membership Trends
   Based on 1968-1996 Data 43

6. Denominational Reports and Other Estimates of Charitable Giving 55

7. Church Member Giving in Perspective:
   Can Religion Influence the Middle Class 67

Appendix A: List of Denominations 79

Appendix B Series: Denominational Data Tables 81
B-1:   Church Member Giving, 1968-1996 83
B-2:   Church Member Giving for 44 Denominations, 1995-1996 94
B-3.1   Church Member Giving for Eleven Denominations,
        1921-1952, in Current Dollars 95
B-3.2   Church Member Giving for Eleven Denominations,
        1953-1967 96
B-3.3   Church Member Giving for Eleven Denominations, The Episcopal
        Church and The United Methodist Church, 1968-1996 100
B-4.1   Membership for Seven Denominations, 1968-1996 101

Appendix C: Income, Deflators, and U.S. Population 102
C.1:   Income and Deflators 103
C.2:   U.S. Population 104

Gratis

98044

Tables and Figures

Table 1   Per Member Giving to Total Contributions,
Congregational Finances and Benevolences,
Current and Inflation-Adjusted 1992 Dollars, 1968-1996 9

Table 2   Per Member Giving as a Percentage of Income, 1968-1996 13

Table 3   Total Contributions, Congregational Finances and
Benevolences, Per Member Giving in Inflation-Adjusted
1992 Dollars, 1968, 1985 and 1996 16

Table 4   Per Member Giving as a Percentage of Income to
Total Contributions, 1968, 1985 and 1996 16

Table 5   Per Member Giving as a Percentage of Income to
Congregational Finances, 1968, 1985 and 1996 17

Table 6   Per Member Giving as a Percentage of Income to
Benevolences, 1968, 1985 and 1996 17

Table 7   Per Member Giving in 44 Denominations, 1995 and 1996,
in Inflation-Adjusted 1992 Dollars and as a Percentage of Income 22

Table 8   Per Member Giving as a Percentage of Income to
Total Contributions, Eight NAE and Seven NCC
Denominations, 1968, 1985 and 1996 27

Table 9   Per Member Giving as a Percentage of Income to
Congregational Finances, Eight NAE and Seven NCC
Denominations, 1968, 1985 and 1996 29

Table 10 Per Member Giving as a Percentage of Income to
Benevolences, Eight NAE and Seven NCC
Denominations, 1968, 1985 and 1996 29

Table 11 Percent Change in Per Member Giving as a Percentage
of Income, Eight NAE and Seven NCC Denominations,
1968 to 1996 31

Table 12 Per Member Giving, Eight NAE and
Seven NCC Denominations, 1968,1985 and 1996,
Inflation-Adjusted 1992 Dollars 32

Table 13 Aggregate Giving, Eight NAE Denominations, 1968
and 1996, in Current and Inflation-Adjusted 1992 Dollars 33

Table 14 Aggregate Giving, Seven NCC Denominations, 1968
and 1996, in Current and Inflation-Adjusted 1992 Dollars 34

Table 15 Average Annual Increase in U.S. Per Capita Income and
Per Member Giving in 11 Denominations, 1950-1996,
Inflation-Adjusted 1992 Dollars 41

Table 16   Giving to Religion, AAFRC Series and Denomination-Based
Series, 1968-1996, Aggregate, Billions of Dollars and
Percent Difference 58

Table 17   AAFRC Giving to Use Categories, 1968 and 1996, Aggregate,
Current and Inflation-Adjusted 1997 Dollars (Billions of Dollars),
and Per Capita as a Percent of U.S. Disposable Personal Income,
with Percent Change 1968-1996 62

Fig. 1   Changes in Per Member Giving in Inflation-Adjusted 1992
Dollars, Total Contributions, Congregational Finances,
and Benevolences, 1968-1996 11

Fig. 2   Per Member Giving to Congregational Finances and Benevolences,
and U.S. Per Capita Personal Income, 1968-1996,
Inflation-Adjusted 1992 Dollars 12

Fig. 3   Per Member Giving as a Percentage of Income to
Congregational Finances and Benevolences, and U.S.
Per Capita Disposable Personal Income, 1968-1996 15

Fig. 4   Per Member Giving as a Percentage of Income to Total
Contributions, Congregational Finances and Benevolences
Eight NAE and Seven NCC Member Denominations,
1968, 1985 and 1996 30

Fig. 5   Per Member Giving to Total Contributions, Congregational Finances
and Benevolences in Eight NAE and Seven NCC Member Denominations, 1968, 1985 and 1996, Inflation-Adjusted 1992 Dollars ... 33

Fig. 6   Per Member Giving as a Percentage of Income in
11 Denominations, and U.S. Per Capita Income, 1921-1996 39

Fig. 7   Trend in Giving as a Percentage of Income to Benevolences,
Composite Denominations, Linear and Exponential Regression
Based on Data for 1968-1985, with Actual Data for 1986-1996 ... 45

Fig. 8   Trend in Giving as a Percentage of Income to Congregational Finances,
Composite Denominations, Linear and Exponential Regression
Based on Data for 1968-1985, with Actual Data for 1986-1996 ... 46

Fig. 9   Giving as a Percentage of Income and Membership as a Percentage
of U.S. Population, Composite Denominations, 1968-1996 47

Fig. 10   Trend in Membership as a Percent of U.S. Population,
Ten Mainline Protestant Denominations, Linear and Exponential
Regression Based on Data for 1968-1985, with
Actual Data for 1986-1996 48

Fig. 11   Trend in Membership as a Percent of U.S. Population,
Composite Denominations, Linear and Exponential Regression
Based on Data for 1968-1995, with Actual Data for 1986-1996 ... 49

Fig. 12   1996 Potential Additional Church Giving, including International
and Domestic Allocations: at a Rate Equal to the Change in U.S.
Per Capita Disposable Personal Income, 1968-1996, and at
a 1996 Average of 10% Giving 53

Fig. 13   Per Capita Giving to Religion, AAFRC Series and Denomination-
Based Series, 1968-1996, as a Percentage of U.S. Per Capita
Disposable Personal Income 61

Fig. 14   AAFRC Use Category Data, 1968-1996 64

Preface

Monitoring and analyzing church member giving patterns impresses one with how important denominational records are. The way church members support their institutions is a clear indicator of their attitudes. Therefore, the faithful work of the many denominational officials who accumulate and aggregate this data is a vital component of this analysis. This year, more than any other, the many demands on these officials' time are apparent. Their willingness to continue sharing of data is all the more valued.

As many scholars and others interested in religious life in the United States know, the *Yearbook of American and Canadian Churches* (YACC) series provides a historical overview of the church in the U.S. throughout this century. Since 1916, yearbook staff have processed and published records from many communions in a single annual volume, making the information available to the general public, church leaders, and academics alike. Credit goes to the leadership of Joan B. Campbell, General Secretary of the National Council of the Churches of Christ in the U.S.A. (NCC), for the NCC's ongoing commitment to this tradition.

Eileen Lindner, the NCC Associate General Secretary for Christian Unity, now serves as YACC editor. She has brought an appreciation of the YACC's historical contribution and a breadth of commitment to the church in the U.S. that has already served to strengthen this series. She is ably assisted in this task by Noah Migel. It is our privilege to work with them, as well as Derek Lander of that office.

Within our own organization, Sarah Sung Yoon Hartmann has been of tremendous help in applying her many talents to the production of this volume. We are also grateful to the staff and supporters of empty tomb, inc. who share a commitment to this work.

Of course, the authors take responsibility for the contents of these pages. The goal is to provide accurate information that gives people a basis for evaluating giving patterns. It is our hope that a fresh look at the facts will contribute to church members fulfilling more of our common potential for loving a hurting world in Jesus' name.

John L. Ronsvalle, Ph.D.
Sylvia Ronsvalle

Champaign, Illinois
December 1998

Summary

The State of Church Giving through 1996 is the most recent report in a series that considers denominational giving data for a set of denominations first analyzed in a study published in 1988. The present report reviews data for 29 denominations from 1968 to 1996 that include 30 million full or confirmed members, and just over 100,000 of the estimated 350,000 religious congregations in the U.S.

The findings of the present church member giving analysis include the following.

- Giving as a percentage of income posted overall declines to Total Contributions and the two subcategories of Congregational Finances and Benevolences between 1968 and 1996. However, by 1996, giving as a percentage of income to Congregational Finances had recovered to 1985 levels. Although giving as a percentage of income to Benevolences continued to decline, the rate of decline slowed from 1995 to 1996.

- When the composite group of 29 denominations was expanded to include a total of 44 Protestant communions, and data was compared for 1995-1996, a decline in giving as a percentage of income to Benevolences was also evident in the expanded set.

- An analysis of data for a subset of mainline Protestant denominations and a subset of evangelical Protestant denominations found giving higher in the evangelical Protestant denominations, but a steeper decline in giving patterns among the evangelicals over the 1968-1996 period. In terms of inflation-adjusted dollars given to Benevolences, both the evangelical and mainline denominations posted a decline on a per member basis between 1985 and 1996, Although the evangelical denominations were increasing in membership during these years, their members were giving a smaller contribution as a portion of income. The mainline denominations increased contributions as a percent of income to Congregational Finances between 1985 and 1996, while a continuing decline to Benevolences was evident.

- A review of giving patterns in 11 Protestant denominations from 1921 to 1996 found per member giving as a portion of income was above 3% from 1922 through 1933, the depth of the Great Depression. It declined in the following years, reaching a low point during World War II. Giving increased through the 1950s, reaching a post-war high of 3.15% in 1960. Giving as a portion of income began to decline in the early 1960s, predating many of the controversial issues often cited as reasons for declines in giving. The 1955-1960 period had the highest ratio of per member giving increase compared to per capita income increase, followed closely by 1950-1955. Two periods, 1947-1968 and 1975-1996, posted 21-years of sustained increase in per member giving in inflation-adjusted dollars.

- Data for 1968-1985 was analyzed using both linear and exponential regression. Then 1986-1996 data was compared to the resulting trends. Both linear and exponential regression closely describe per member giving as a portion of income to Benevolences. Congregational Finances more closely resembled the exponential curve. Membership as a portion of U.S. population in 10 mainline denominations was best described by an exponential curve, while membership as a portion of U.S. population for the 29 denominations resembled the linear regression trend more closely. The potential for church giving levels was calculated: at the rate of income increase from 1968 to 1996; and at an average of 10% giving in 1996. The results suggested that church members have sizable resources available, in theory, to apply to domestic and global needs. However, the data in the earlier chapters suggests church members have displayed no signs of improving giving patterns.

- The annual rate of change in the data set of 29 denominations was used to develop a total giving to religion series keyed to the 1974 Filer Commission estimate of giving to religion. This series was compared to the American Association of Fund Raising Counsel, Inc. (AAFRC) *Giving USA* series. The AAFRC series includes data for years when AAFRC added to religion any difference between their total giving estimate and the sum of its use category estimates. The AAFRC series was higher than the denomination-based series. This finding had implications for individual giving and total giving as well.

- The final chapter presents a discussion of the integration of religious profession and practice. The question asked is, "Can religion influence the middle class?" Two surveys—one looking at the ethics of young people, and the other the values of adults—are considered. In addition, a brief review of consumer spending is presented.

Introduction

How does one accumulate data for approximately 100,000 of the estimated 350,000 religious organizations in the United States?

The individual congregations initially provided the data to the regional or national denominational office with which the congregation is affiliated. The denominational offices then compiled the data. The Yearbook of American and Canadian *Churches* (*YACC*), of the National Council of the Churches of Christ in the U.S.A., requested the data from the national denominational offices, publishing it in the annual YACC editions.

The data published by the *YACC*, in some cases combined with data obtained directly from a denominational source (as noted in the series of tables in Appendix B), serves as the basis for the present report. The numbers on the following pages are not survey reports. Rather, they represent the records turned in by pastors to their own denominational offices.

By following the same data set over a period of years, trends can be seen among a particular set of church members. In addition, since the data set includes communions from across the theological spectrum, subsets of denominations within the larger grouping provide a basis for comparing patterns between communions with different perspectives.

Efforts are continually being made to use the latest information available. As a result, several analysis factors have been revised in *The State of Church Giving through 1996* (see the section titled "Revised Analysis Factors" below).

Definition of Terms. The analyses in this report use certain terms that are defined as follows.

Full or Confirmed Members are used in the present analysis because it is a relatively consistent category among the reporting denominations. Certain denominations also report a larger figure for Inclusive Membership, which may include, for example, children who have been baptized but are not yet eligible for confirmation in that denomination. In this report, when the term "per member" is used, it refers to Full or Confirmed Members, unless otherwise noted.

Total Contributions Per Member refers to the average contribution in either dollars or as a percentage of income which is donated to the denominations' affiliated congregations by Full or Confirmed Members in a given year.

Total Contributions combines two subcategories of Congregational Finances and Benevolences. The definitions used in this report for the two subcategories are consistent with the standardized *YACC* data request questionnaire.

The first subcategory is Congregational Finances, which includes all contributions directed to the internal operation of the individual congregation, including such items as the utility bills and salaries for the pastor and office staff, as well as Sunday school materials and capital programs.

The other subcategory is Benevolences. This category includes contributions for the congregation's external expenditures, beyond its own operations, for what might be termed the larger mission of the church. Benevolences includes international missions as well as national and local charities, through denominational channels as well as programs of nondenominational organizations to which the congregation contributes directly. Benevolences also includes support of denomination administration at all levels, as well as donations to denominational seminaries and schools. It may be noted that in the case of one denomination considered in chapters two and four, the category includes pastoral medical insurance and pension payments.

As those familiar with congregational dynamics know, an individual generally donates an amount to the congregation which is then divided between these two subcategories by the congregational leadership during the budget preparation process. The budget may or may not be approved by all the congregation's members, depending on the communion's polity. However, the sum of the congregation's activities serves as the basis for members' decisions about whether to increase or decrease giving from one year to the next. Also, many congregations provide opportunities to designate directly to either Congregational Finances or Benevolences, through fund-raising drives, capital campaigns, and special offerings. Therefore, the allocations between Congregational Finances and Benevolences can be seen to fairly represent the priorities of church members.

When the terms "income," "per capita income," and "giving as a percentage of income" are used, they refer to the U.S. Department of Commerce Bureau of Economic Analysis' U.S. Per Capita Disposable (after-tax) Personal Income series, unless otherwise noted.

The Implicit Price Deflator for Gross National Product was used to convert current dollars to 1992 dollars, thus factoring out inflation, unless otherwise specified (see "Revised Analysis Factors" section below).

Appendix C includes both U.S. Per Capita Disposable Personal Income figures and the Implicit Price Deflator for Gross National Product figures used in this study.

Revised Analysis Factors. In October 1995, the U.S. Bureau of Economic Analysis (U.S. BEA) issued revised tables for implicit price deflators. These tables were part of a comprehensive revision that affected three factors used in The State of Church Giving series: deflators, chained dollars, and income series. As a result, the analyses in *The State of Church Giving through 1995* revised and updated findings in the earlier editions.

Chained Dollars. The U.S. BEA issued a comprehensive revision, including a change from "constant 1987 dollars" to "chained (1992) dollars." The revised figures provide " 'chain-type annual-weighted' measures."[1] The benchmark year was changed from 1987 to 1992 "because that is the latest year for which the current-dollar estimates will not be subject to revision until the next comprehensive revision."[2]

Income Series. The U.S. Department of Commerce Bureau of Economic Analysis (U.S. BEA) has been in the process of publishing a revised income series, in conjunction with its comprehensive revision. The U.S. Per Capita Disposable Personal Income data used in the present *The State of Church Giving through 1996* includes a revised 1929-1981 series that was published by the U.S. BEA in 1998. The revised 1982 through 1996 series was published by the U.S. BEA in August of 1998. Because of these income revisions, the information in The State of Church Giving *through 1996* is not strictly comparable with previous editions in the series.

Rate of Change Calculations, 1985-1996. The following methodology is used to calculate the rate of change between 1985 and the most recent calendar year, which in the present case is 1996.

The rate of change between 1968 and 1985 was calculated by subtracting the 1968 giving as a percentage of income figure from the 1985 figure and then dividing the result by the 1968 figure.

The rate of change between 1985 and 1996 was calculated as follows. The 1968 giving as a percentage of income figure was subtracted from the 1996 figure and divided by the 1968 figure, producing a 1968-1996 rate of change. Then, the 1968-1985 rate of change was subtracted from the 1968-1996 figure. The result is the 1985-1996 rate of change, which may then be compared to the 1968-1985 figure.

Rounding Calculations. In most cases, Total Contributions, Total Congregational Finances, and Total Benevolences for the denominations being considered were divided by Full or Confirmed Membership in order to obtain per capita, or per member, data for that set of denominations. This procedure occasionally led to a small rounding discrepancy in one of the three related figures. That is, by a small margin, rounded per capita Total Contributions did not equal per capita Congregational Finances plus per capita Benevolences. Similarly, rounding data to the nearest dollar for use in tables and graphics led on occasion to a small rounding error in the data presented in tabular or graphic form.

Giving in Dollars. Per member giving to churches can be measured in dollars. The dollar measure indicates, among other information, how much money religious institutions have to spend. Did congregations have as much to spend in 1996 as they did in 1968? This question can be considered in both current dollars and inflation-adjusted dollars.

Current dollars indicate the value of the dollar in the year it was donated. However, since inflation changes the amount of goods or services that can be purchased with that dollar, data provided in current dollars has limited information value over a time span. If someone donated $5 in 1968 and $5 in 1996, on one level that person is donating the same amount of money. On another level, however, the buying power of that $5 has changed a great deal.

---

[1] *Survey of Current Business*, October 1995, page 30.
[2] *Survey of Current Business*, October 1995, page 30, footnote 3.

Since less can be bought with the $5 donated in 1996 because of inflation in the economy, on a practical level the value of the donation has shrunk.

To account for the changes caused by inflation in the value of the dollar, a deflator can be applied. The result is inflation-adjusted 1992 dollars. Dollars adjusted to their chain-type, annual-weighted measure through the use of a deflator can be compared in terms of real growth over a time span since inflation has been factored out.

The deflator most commonly applied in this analysis designated the base period as 1992, with levels in 1992 set equal to 100. Thus, when adjusted by the deflator, the 1968 gift of $5 was worth $18.08 in inflation-adjusted 1992 dollars, and the 1996 gift of $5 was worth $4.57 in inflation-adjusted 1992 dollars.

Giving as a Percentage of Income. There is another way to look at church member giving. This category is giving as a percentage of income. Considering what percentage or portion of income is donated to the religious congregation provides a different perspective. Rather than indicating how much money the congregation has to spend, as when one considers dollars donated, giving as a percentage of income indicates how the congregation rates in light of church members' total available incomes. Has the church sustained the same level of support from its members in comparison to previous years, as measured by what portion of income is being donated by members from the total resources available to them?

Percentage of income is a valuable measure because incomes change. Just as inflation changes the value of the dollar, so that $5 in 1968 is not the same as $5 in 1996, incomes, influenced by inflation and real growth, also change. For example, per capita income in 1968 was $3,101 in current dollars; if a church member gave $310 that year, that member would have been tithing, or giving the standard of ten percent. In contrast, 1996 per capita income had increased to $20,840 in current dollars; and if that church member still gave $310, the member would have been giving only 1.5% of income. The church would have commanded a smaller portion of the member's overall financial activity.

Thus, while dollars donated indicate how much the church has to spend, giving as a percentage of income provides some measure of the church member's level of commitment to the church in comparison to other spending priorities. One might say that giving as a percentage of income is an indication of the church's "market share" of church members' lives.

In most cases, to obtain giving as a percentage of income, total income to a set of denominations was divided by the number of Full or Confirmed Members in the set. This yielded the per member giving amount in dollars. This per member giving amount was divided by per capita income.

Data Appendix and Revisions. Appendix B includes the denominational data used in the analyses in this study. In general, the data for the denominations included in these analyses appears as it was reported in editions of the *YACC*. In some cases, data for one or more years for a specific denomination was obtained directly from the denominational office or another denominational source. Also, the denominational giving data set has been refined and revised as additional information has become available. Where relevant, this information is noted in the appendix.

1

Church Member Giving, 1968-1996_____

History is easier to read than to live.

The advantage of thumbing through a printed volume is that of hindsight which, as conventional wisdom notes, permits 20/20 vision.

In the midst of life, as history is being written by our everyday choices, the bigger implications of the small decisions we make are, many times, hard to perceive. Individual actions do not seem to carry major consequences. People may feel powerless to affect their larger surroundings. So they focus on the immediate. Yet it is the combination of these small individual decisions that ultimately defines how history will read years from now.

In this context, studying church member giving patterns becomes more than a discussion of whether the institutional church has enough money to keep the lights on. The church continues to be a major social institution in the United States. The choices in spending habits made by individuals affiliated with that institution provide one standard by which to judge the church's influence. Is members' giving to the church in keeping with their faith's traditional stated convictions? Or is there a difference between what people say and what people do about their religion?

Church member giving patterns are one indicator of the integration of the stated faith and the practiced faith. Religious traditions generally teach that it is the responsibility of believers to support their institutions. Some, including the Judeo-Christian tradition, also teach that there is an additional component of giving that sits in the context of a relationship to God, and that serves as a way to support what God cares about.

The portion of income given, then, can serve as a gauge of the value church members place on their religious practices.

Measuring financial donations is possible because of records accumulated and published by the *Yearbook of American and Canadian Churches* (*YACC*). Tracking giving patterns in a set of denominations provides one basis to review how the church is faring, compared to other areas in which church members also invest their lives.

Twenty-nine Denominations. The first study that provided a basis for the present series was published in 1988. It considered a set of 31 denominations which provided church member giving data for 1968 and 1985 in the *Yearbook of American and Canadian Churches*

(*YACC*) series that could be confirmed.[1] The data year 1968 was selected because, beginning that year, a consistent distinction was made between Full or Confirmed Membership and Inclusive Membership in the *YACC* series. The denominations that published data for both 1968 and 1985 included 29,442,390 Full or Confirmed Members in 1985. They comprise approximately 100,000 of the estimated 350,000 religious congregations in the U.S.

The present church member giving report series extended the analysis for the original set of denominations beyond 1985. The current report analyzes the data set, now comprising 29 denominations, through 1996, the most recent year for which data was available at the time the report was written.[2] Also, data for the intervening years of 1969 through 1984, and 1986 through 1995, was included in the composite data set, as available.[3]

In reviewing church member giving, at least two approaches can be taken. First, the number of dollars given by members indicates how much money the church has to spend. It can also be compared to other dollar expenditures for various consumer items, as is done in the last chapter of this volume. However, the number of dollars given do not take into account the level of changing resources available to the church member.

Giving as a percentage of income, on the other hand, places donations in the larger context of income available to church members. Incomes change by both inflation, but also real growth. Church members in the mid-1990s were deciding how much to give from a different income base than did people in the late 1960s. In 1996, were church members directing the same portion of their incomes to their churches as did members three decades ago? The percentage of income gives a measure of the church's "market share" of members' lifestyles.

Church Giving in Current Dollars. Calculating contributions on a per member basis accounts for any changes in membership, either through growth or decline, that might have taken place during the period under review. The number of dollars donated by members indicates how much the church had to spend on both local institutional operations, as well as what might be termed its larger mission.

---

[1]John Ronsvalle and Sylvia Ronsvalle, *A Comparison of the Growth in Church Contributions with United States Per Capita Income* (Champaign, IL: empty tomb, inc., 1988).

[2]Two of the original 31 denominations merged in 1987, bringing the total number of denominations in the original data set to 30. As of 1991, one denomination reported that it no longer had the staff to collect national financial data, resulting in a maximum of 29 denominations from the original set which could provide data for 1991 through 1996. One of these 29 denominations did not have comprehensive financial information at the time the present report was drafted, but hopes to in time for the next edition. Therefore, throughout this report, what was an original set of 31 denominations in 1985 will be referred to as a set of 29 denominations, reflecting the denominations' 1995 composition, although data for 31 denominations will be included for 1968 and 1985, as well as for intervening years, as available.

[3]For 1986 through 1996, annual denominational data has been obtained which represented for any given year at least 99.31% of the 1985 Full or Confirmed Membership of the denominations included in the 1968-1985 study. The number of denominations for which data was available varied from a low of 25 in 1986 to a high of 29 in 1991 through 1995. The denominational giving data considered in this analysis was obtained either from the *Yearbook of American and Canadian Churches* series, or directly in correspondence with a denominational office. For a full listing of the data used in this analysis, including the sources, see Appendix B-1.

One major factor must be considered when reviewing giving in terms of dollar amounts. Because inflation affects the value of dollars, a dollar in 1996 bought fewer goods or services than it did in 1968, much to the professed surprise of many churchgoers.

In order to account for this factor, giving in dollars can be considered from two points of view: current dollars (the value the dollars had in the year they were donated); and inflation-adjusted dollars, factoring out the economic impact of inflation.

Table 1 presents the data for the per member contribution in dollars for the composite group of denominations included in the data set in both current and inflation-adjusted dollars.

Table 1: **Per Member Giving to Total Contributions, Congregational Finances and Benevolences, Current and Inflation-Adjusted 1992 Dollars, 1968-1996**

Per Full or Confirmed Member Giving to Congregations, in Dollars								
	Current Dollars			Inflation-Adjusted 1992 Dollars				
Year	Total	Cong. Finances	Benevol.	Total	↑↓	Cong. Finances	↑↓	Benevol.	↑↓
1968	$96.60	$76.24	$20.37	$349.26		$275.62		$73.64	
1969	$100.63	$79.04	$21.59	$347.49	↓	$272.94	↓	$74.56	↑
1970	$104.10	$82.67	$21.43	$341.30	↓	$271.05	↓	$70.25	↓
1971	$109.50	$86.98	$22.52	$341.33	↑	$271.13	↑	$70.20	↓
1972	$116.97	$93.13	$23.84	$349.80	↑	$278.50	↑	$71.29	↑
1973	$127.32	$101.95	$25.37	$360.47	↑	$288.65	↑	$71.82	↑
1974	$138.77	$110.67	$28.10	$360.54	↑	$287.54	↓	$73.00	↑
1975	$150.00	$118.24	$31.76	$356.22	↓	$280.80	↓	$75.42	↑
1976	$162.69	$128.94	$33.75	$364.95	↑	$289.23	↑	$75.71	↑
1977	$175.52	$139.90	$35.62	$369.83	↑	$294.77	↑	$75.06	↓
1978	$192.65	$154.34	$38.30	$378.34	↑	$303.11	↑	$75.22	↑
1979	$211.21	$169.25	$41.96	$382.22	↑	$306.28	↑	$75.93	↑
1980	$232.12	$185.77	$46.35	$384.56	↑	$307.76	↑	$76.79	↑
1981	$255.24	$204.12	$51.12	$386.44	↑	$309.05	↑	$77.39	↑
1982	$275.89	$223.37	$52.52	$392.95	↑	$318.15	↑	$74.81	↓
1983	$292.78	$236.65	$56.13	$399.97	↑	$323.29	↑	$76.68	↑
1984	$315.46	$256.44	$59.02	$415.25	↑	$337.56	↑	$77.69	↑
1985	$335.69	$272.63	$63.07	$427.26	↑	$346.98	↑	$80.27	↑
1986	$354.19	$288.15	$66.04	$439.34	↑	$357.42	↑	$81.92	↑
1987	$367.85	$301.32	$66.53	$442.71	↑	$362.65	↑	$80.07	↓
1988	$382.35	$312.56	$69.79	$443.97	↑	$362.93	↑	$81.04	↑
1989	$403.60	$330.79	$72.81	$449.69	↑	$368.57	↑	$81.12	↑
1990	$420.17	$346.16	$74.01	$448.76	↓	$369.71	↑	$79.04	↓
1991	$434.32	$358.60	$75.73	$446.24	↓	$368.43	↓	$77.81	↓
1992	$445.90	$368.19	$77.71	$445.90	↓	$368.19	↓	$77.71	↓
1993	$458.38	$380.47	$77.91	$446.63	↑	$370.72	↑	$75.91	↓
1994	$489.66	$409.26	$80.40	$465.99	↑	$389.48	↑	$76.51	↑
1995	$512.54	$429.91	$82.63	$476.83	↑	$399.96	↑	$76.87	↑
1996	$538.33	$452.51	$85.81	$491.62	↑	$413.25	↑	$78.37	↑

Details in the above table may not compute to the numbers shown due to rounding.

Each data series is considered in three categories. Total Contributions Per Member represents the average total contribution for each full or confirmed church member in the composite 29 denominations. This Total Contributions figure combines two subcategories: Congregational Finances (which includes the monies the congregation spent on internal operations); and Benevolences (which includes what might be termed the larger mission of the church, such as local, national and international missions, as well as denominational support and seminary funding, among other items).

It may be noted that the per member amount given to Total Contributions increased in current dollars each year during the 1968-1996 period. The portion of Total Contributions Per Member which stayed in the congregation to fund Congregational Finances also went up each year. In this same period, current dollar per member contributions to Benevolences declined only once, from 1969 to 1970. Otherwise, giving to Benevolences also increased each year.

Overall, from 1968 to 1996, Total Contributions to the church in current dollars increased $441.72 on a per member basis. Of this amount, $376.28 was directed to increase the per member Congregational Finances expenditures, for the benefit of members within the congregation. Benevolences, or outreach, activities of the congregation, increased by $65.45 (rounded numbers). On a current dollar basis, 15% of the total increase from 1968 to 1996 was directed to Benevolences.

One effect of this allocation was that Benevolences shrank as a portion of Total Contributions. In 1968, 21¢ of each dollar went to Benevolences. By 1996, the amount had decreased to 16¢. Further, when inflation was factored out, it becomes clear that churches were carrying out Benevolences in 1996 with only a slightly higher level of resources than those available to fund these activities in 1968.

Church Giving in Inflation-Adjusted Dollars. The U.S. Bureau of Economic Analysis (U.S. BEA) periodically revises the deflator series that are used to factor out inflation. These deflators allow dollar figures to be compared more precisely across years. The U.S. BEA issued such a deflator series revision in the mid-1990s. The year of base comparison was changed from 1987 to 1992. Further, a change was made from the concept of "constant" dollars to "chained" dollars.[4] By applying the revised implicit price deflator to the current dollar church member giving data, the data can be reviewed across years with inflation factored out. The result of this process is also listed in Table 1. The arrows next to the three inflation-adjusted columns are intended to provide an easy reference as to whether giving increased or decreased from one year to the next.

When the effects of inflation are removed in the 1968 to 1996 giving amounts, one may note that per member giving decreased in more years than in the current dollar columns. For example, although per member contributions to Total Contributions increased in the majority of years, the years 1969, 1970, 1975, and a three-year period from 1990 to 1992 posted declines.

Congregational Finances also generally increased in inflation-adjusted 1992 dollars. Six exceptions were the years 1969, 1970, 1974, 1975, and a two-year period from 1991 to 1992.

---

[4]See the section titled "Revised Analysis Factors" in the Introduction for further detail.

Benevolences also increased in the majority of years. Nevertheless, decreases may be observed nine times in the 1968-1996 interval, in the years 1970, 1971, 1977, 1982, 1987, and the four years from 1990 to 1993.

Figure 1 presents the changes in inflation-adjusted dollar contributions to the three categories of Total Contributions, Congregational Finances and Benevolences.

Figure 1: **Changes in Per Member Giving in Inflation-Adjusted 1992 Dollars, Total Contributions, Congregational Finances, and Benevolences, 1968-1996**

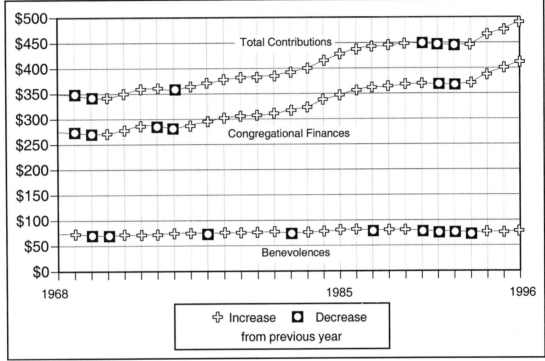

Sources: *Yearbook of American and Canadian Churches,* adjusted series; U.S. Bureau of Economic Analysis

empty tomb, inc. 1998

Over the 1968-1996 period, per member donations to Total Contributions in inflation-adjusted dollars increased from $349.26 to $491.62, an increase of $142.36, or 41%.

Of the total increase, $137.63 was directed to Congregational Finances. This subcategory increased 50% between 1968 and 1996, from $275.62 to $413.25.

In contrast, Benevolences increased $4.73, from $73.64 in 1968 to $78.37 in 1996. Thus, Benevolences increased an average of 6% per member between 1968 and 1996.

Of the total inflation-adjusted dollar increase between 1968 and 1996, 97% was directed to Congregational Finances. This emphasis on the internal operations of the congregation helps explain the finding that Benevolences represented 21% of all church activity in 1968, and 16% in 1996.

Figure 2 provides a comparison of per member giving to the categories of Congregational Finances and Benevolences with changes in U.S. per capita disposable personal income in inflation-adjusted 1992 dollars.

Figure 2: **Per Member Giving to Congregational Finances and Benevolences, and U.S. Per Capita Personal Income, 1968-1996, Inflation-Adjusted 1992 Dollars**

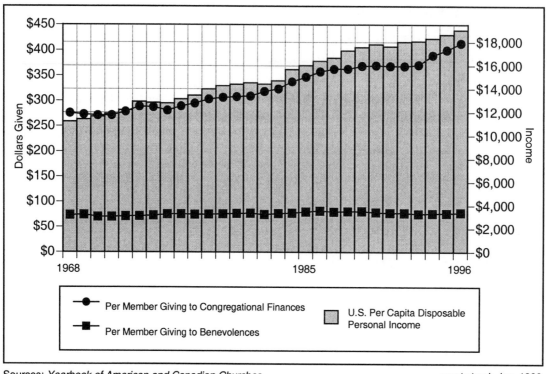

Sources: *Yearbook of American and Canadian Churches*, adjusted series; U.S. Bureau of Economic Analysis

empty tomb, inc. 1998

Giving as a Percent of Income. U.S. per capita disposable (after-tax) personal income serves as an average income figure for the broad spectrum of church members included in the composite of 29 denominations.

U.S. per capita disposable personal income was $3,101 in current dollars in 1968. When that figure is calculated in inflation-adjusted 1992 dollars, U.S. per capita disposable personal income in 1968 was $11,211.

The current-dollar income figure for 1996 was $20,840. When inflation was factored out, 1996 U.S. per capita disposable personal income was $19,032.

Thus, per capita income in inflation-adjusted dollars increased by $7,821, an increase of 70% from 1968 to 1996.

In Table 2, giving as a percentage of income is presented for per member Total Contributions, and the related subcategories of Congregational Finances and Benevolences. As in Table 1 the arrows indicate whether the percentage of income in that category increased or decreased from the previous year. Inasmuch as the percent figures are rounded to the second decimal place, the arrows indicate the direction of a slight increase or decrease for those situations in which the percentage provided appears to be the same numerical figure as the previous year.

Table 2:   **Per Member Giving as a Percentage of Income, 1968-1996**

Per Full or Confirmed Member Giving to Congregations as a Percentage of Income						
Year	Total Contributions Per Member	↑↓	Congregational Finances	↑↓	Benevolences	↑↓
1968	3.12%		2.46%		0.66%	
1969	3.05%	↓	2.39%	↓	0.65%	↓
1970	2.93%	↓	2.33%	↓	0.60%	↓
1971	2.87%	↓	2.28%	↓	0.59%	↓
1972	2.87%	↓	2.28%	↓	0.58%	↓
1973	2.79%	↓	2.23%	↓	0.56%	↓
1974	2.81%	↑	2.24%	↑	0.57%	↑
1975	2.79%	↓	2.20%	↓	0.59%	↑
1976	2.78%	↓	2.20%	↑	0.58%	↓
1977	2.75%	↓	2.19%	↓	0.56%	↓
1978	2.70%	↓	2.17%	↓	0.54%	↓
1979	2.68%	↓	2.15%	↓	0.53%	↓
1980	2.67%	↓	2.14%	↓	0.53%	↑
1981	2.66%	↓	2.13%	↓	0.53%	↓
1982	2.72%	↑	2.20%	↑	0.52%	↓
1983	2.72%	↓	2.20%	↓	0.52%	↑
1984	2.65%	↓	2.15%	↓	0.50%	↓
1985	2.67%	↑	2.17%	↑	0.50%	↑
1986	2.68%	↑	2.18%	↑	0.50%	↓
1987	2.66%	↓	2.18%	↓	0.48%	↓
1988	2.57%	↓	2.10%	↓	0.47%	↓
1989	2.56%	↓	2.10%	↓	0.46%	↓
1990	2.52%	↓	2.07%	↓	0.44%	↓
1991	2.53%	↑	2.09%	↑	0.44%	↓
1992	2.47%	↓	2.04%	↓	0.43%	↓
1993	2.47%	↓	2.05%	↑	0.42%	↓
1994	2.54%	↑	2.13%	↑	0.42%	↓
1995	2.56%	↑	2.14%	↑	0.41%	↓
1996	2.58%	↑	2.17%	↑	0.41%	↓

Details in the above table may not compute to the numbers shown due to rounding.

While Table 1 presents data in both current and inflation-adjusted dollars, Table 2 lists a single set of data for giving as a percentage of income. There is no distinction between current or inflation-adjusted dollars when one is considering giving as a percentage of income. The same procedures are applied to both the giving and income dollar amounts when converting current dollars into inflation-adjusted dollars. As long as one compares current dollar giving to current dollar per capita income when calculating the percentage of income, and inflation-adjusted dollar giving to inflation-adjusted dollar per capita income while using the same deflator, the percentages of income will be the same.

A review of Table 2 yields the following information.

Overall, per member giving as a percentage of income to Total Contributions decreased from 3.12% to 2.58%, a decline of 17%. Giving as a percentage of income to Total Contributions decreased 20 times out of a possible 28 times.

The trends differ from giving in dollars. The review of the dollar numbers in Table 1 indicated that per member giving increased in both current and inflation-adjusted dollars. However, when that dollar giving is considered in light of changes to income, a different picture emerges. While church members increased the amount of dollars they donated to the church between 1968 through 1996, the rate of increase in the number of dollars donated was not comparable to the rate of increase in U.S. per capita income. Per member Total Contributions increased 41% in inflation-adjusted dollars from 1968 to 1996. However, U.S. per capita disposable personal income increased 70% during the same period.

The difference in the rate of increase between dollars contributed and per capita income explains how church member contributions could be increasing in inflation-adjusted dollars in most of the years from 1968 to 1996, and yet decreasing as a percentage of income in most of the years from 1968 to 1996.

Evaluating the dollars donated in the context of changes in income results in the finding that the portion of income members directed to their churches decreased by 17% during the 1968 to 1996 period. One conclusion would be that the church's influence on members' priorities appeared to be weakening. However, most recently from 1994 to 1996, the portion of per member income given to Total Contributions increased three years in a row, the longest sustained increase in the 1968-1996 period.

Congregational Finances decreased 18 times during the 28 two-year sets in the 1968-1996 period. There were two five-year periods of decline, from 1969 to 1973, and from 1977 to 1981. There was also a four-year period when declines were posted from 1987 to 1990. Congregational Finances declined from 2.46% in 1968 to 2.17% in 1996, a percent change of -12% from the 1968 base in giving as a percentage of income. The most recent four-year period, from 1993 to 1996, is the longest period of increase in the 1968-1996 period.

Benevolences declined from 0.66% of income in 1968 to 0.41% in 1996, a decline of 37% in the portion of income that was directed to Benevolences. Out of the 28 two-year sets in the 1968-1996 interval, the portion of income that went to Benevolences declined 23 times. Although there were five years in a row, from 1969 to 1973, that posted decreases in Benevolences, the longest uninterrupted decline occurred in the eleven data years from 1986 through 1996.

Figure 3 presents per member giving as a percentage of income to Congregational Finances and Benevolences, compared to U.S. per capita income.

Giving in Constant Dollars, 1968, 1985 and 1996. The first report, that served as the basis for the present series on church member giving, considered data for the denominations in the composite for the years 1968 and 1985. With the data now available through 1996, a broader trend can be reviewed for the period under discussion, the 29-year range from 1968 to 1996.

The per member amount donated to Total Contributions in inflation-adjusted 1992 dollars was $78.00 greater in 1985 than it was in 1968 for the denominations included in the

Figure 3: **Per Member Giving as a Percentage of Income to Congregational Finances and Benevolences, and U.S. Per Capita Disposable Personal Income, 1968-1996**

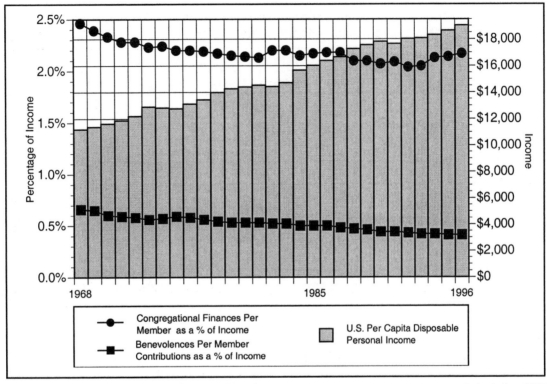

Sources: *Yearbook of American and Canadian Churches,* adjusted series; U.S. Bureau of Economic Analysis

empty tomb, inc. 1998

data set, an average increase of $4.59 a year in per member contributions. There was an overall increase during the 1985-1996 eleven-year interval as well. In 1996, the per member contribution to the 29 denominations, which represented 99.31% of the total 1985 membership of the denominations originally studied, was $64.37 more per member in inflation-adjusted dollars than in 1985. The average annual increase was $5.85 between 1985 and 1996, a higher rate compared to the 1968-1985 average annual increase of $4.59.

Gifts to Congregational Finances also increased between 1968 and 1985, as well as from 1985 to 1996. As in the case of Total Contributions, the annual rate of increase accelerated. Per member contributions to Congregational Finances were $275.62 in 1968, in inflation-adjusted 1992 dollars, and had increased to $346.98 in 1985, a total increase of $71.36, with an average rate of change of $4.20. From 1985 to 1996, the average annual rate of change increased to $6.02, with per member gifts growing from $346.98 in 1985 to $413.25 in 1996, an increase of $66.27.

Benevolences experienced a reversal in the rate of change during the 1985 to 1996 period. In inflation-adjusted 1992 dollars, gifts to Benevolences were $73.64 in 1968 and grew to $80.27 in 1985, an increase of $6.64, with an annual average rate of change of $0.39. Between 1985 and 1996, per member gifts to Benevolences declined to $78.37 in 1996 from the 1985 level of $80.27, a decrease of $1.90, with an annual average rate of change of -$0.17 for the 1985-1996 period.

15

Table 3 presents per member gifts to Total Contributions, Congregational Finances and Benevolences in inflation-adjusted 1992 dollars for the years 1968, 1985 and 1996.

Table 3: **Total Contributions, Congregational Finances and Benevolences, Per Member Giving in Inflation-Adjusted 1992 Dollars, 1968, 1985 and 1996**

Per Member Giving in Inflation-Adjusted 1992 Dollars								
	Total Contributions			Congregational Finances			Benevolences		
Year	Per Member Giving in Adjusted '92 Dollars	Diff. from Previous $ Base	Average Annual Diff. in $s Given	Per Member Giving in Adjusted '92 Dollars	Diff. from Previous $ Base	Average Annual Diff. in $s Given	Per Member Giving in Adjusted '92 Dollars	Diff. from Previous $ Base	Average Annual Diff. in $s Given
1968	$349.26			$275.62			$73.64		
1985	$427.26	$78.00	$4.59	$346.98	$71.36	$4.20	$80.27	$6.64	$0.39
1996	$491.62	$64.37	$5.85	$413.25	$66.27	$6.02	$78.37	-$1.90	-$0.17

Details in the above table may not compute to the numbers shown due to rounding.

Giving as a Percentage of Income, 1968, 1985 and 1996. Between 1968 and 1985, Total Contributions declined from 3.12% to 2.67% as a portion of income. The percentage change in giving as a percentage of income from the 1968 base was -14.42% in the 17 years from 1968 to 1985.

From 1985 to 1996, giving as a percentage of income to Total Contributions changed from 2.67% in 1985 to 2.58% in 1996. The percentage change in giving as a percentage of income was -2.66% in this eleven-year interval. Therefore, the annual percent change in the portion of per capita income donated to Total Contributions was -0.24% in the 1985-1996 period, compared to the rate of -0.85% in the 1968-1985 period. This data suggests that the rate of annual decline in giving as a percentage of income decreased in the last eleven years of the 1968 to 1996 period.

Table 4 presents data for Total Contributions Per member as a percentage of income in summary fashion for the years 1968, 1985 and 1996.

Table 4: **Per Member Giving as a Percentage of Income to Total Contributions, 1968, 1985 and 1996[5]**

Total Contributions Per Member as a Percentage of Income				
Year	Total Contributions Per Member as a Percentage of Income	Difference in Total Contributions Per Member as a Percentage of Income from Previous Base	Percent Change in Total Contributions Per Member as % of Income Calculated from 1968 Base	Annual Average Percent Change in Total Contributions Per Member as a Percentage of Income
1968	3.12%			
1985	2.67%	-0.45%	-14.42% from 1968	-0.85%
1996	2.58%	- 0.09%	- 2.66% from 1985	- 0.24%

Details in the above table may not compute to the numbers shown due to rounding.

---

[5]See the explanation in the Introduction as to how the 1968-1985 and 1985-1995 rates of change were calculated.

Per member gifts to Congregational Finances measured 2.46% of income in 1968, 2.17% in 1985 and 2.17% in 1996. The annual average percent change in giving as a percentage of income changed from -0.70% a year between 1968 and 1985, from the 1968 base, to 0.02% a year between 1985 and 1996. The data indicates a reversal in the annual rate of change in giving as a percentage of income to Congregational Finances in the last eleven years of the 1968-1996 period. Data in future years will indicate whether the rate of change in giving to Congregational Finances has stabilized or may begin to demonstrate a sustained increase. Table 5 presents this data.

Table 5: **Per Member Giving as a Percentage of Income to Congregational Finances, 1968, 1985 and 1996**

Congregational Finances Per Member as a Percentage of Income				
Year	Cong. Finances Per Member as a Percentage of Income	Difference in Cong. Finances Per Member as a Percentage of Income from Previous Base	Percent Change in Cong. Finances Per Member as % of Income Calculated from 1968 Base	Annual Average Percent Change in Cong. Finances Per Member as a Percentage of Income
1968	2.46%			
1985	2.17%	-0.29%	-11.93% from 1968	-0.70%
1996	2.17%	0%	0.26% from 1985	0.02%

Details in the above table may not compute to the numbers shown due to rounding.

Table 6 presents the data for Benevolences as a percentage of income in 1968, 1985 and 1996. Between 1985 and 1996, the annual average percent decline in giving as a percentage of income to Benevolences was smaller than that during the 1968-1985 period. From 1968 to 1985, the portion of member income directed to Benevolences decreased from 0.66% to 0.50%, an absolute decline of -0.16%. This figure translated to a percent change in giving as a percentage of income of -23.74% from the 1968 base, with an annual average percent change of -1.40%. In the eleven-year interval from 1985 to 1996, giving as a percentage of income directed to Benevolences declined from 0.50% to 0.41% between 1985 and 1996, an absolute drop of 0.09% during those eleven years, compared to a decline of

Table 6: **Per Member Giving as a Percentage of Income to Benevolences, 1968, 1985 and 1996**

Benevolences Per Member as a Percentage of Income				
Year	Benevolences Per Member as a Percentage of Income	Difference in Benevolences Per Member as a Percentage of Income from Previous Base	Percent Change in Benevolences Per Member as % of Income Calculated from 1968 Base	Annual Average Percent Change in Benevolences Per Member as a Percentage of Income
1968	0.66%			
1985	0.50%	-0.16%	-23.74% from 1968	-1.40%
1996	0.41%	- 0.09%	- 13.56% from 1985	- 1.23%

Details in the above table may not compute to the numbers shown due to rounding.

0.16% in the 17-year interval of 1968-1985. The 1985-1996 percent change in giving as a percentage of income of -13.56% produced an annual average percent change of -1.23%, indicating an improvement from the 1968-1985 seventeen-year rate of -1.40%.

Giving in 1995 Compared to 1996. Per member giving as a percentage of income to Total Contributions in 1995 measured 2.56%. In 1996, the figure was 2.58%.

Congregational Finances also improved from 1995 to 1996, from 2.14% in 1995 to 2.17% in 1996.

From 1995 to 1996, Benevolences extended a multiyear pattern of decline. Although the level of giving rounded to 0.41% of income in both years, the unrounded numbers suggested a slight decline from 1995 to 1996.

Potential Giving. Apart from the question of whether church members could have been giving a higher percentage of their incomes in 1996 than in 1968, what would have been the situation in 1996 if giving had at least maintained the 1968 percentages of income donated? Rather than the actual 1996 levels of giving, what if giving as a percentage of income in 1996 measured 3.12% for Total Contributions, 2.46% for Congregational Finances, and 0.66% for Benevolences, which were the levels of giving for these three categories in 1968?

Had that been true, per member giving to Total Contributions in current 1996 dollars would have been $649.43 instead of $538.33; Congregational Finances would have been $512.84 instead of $452.51; and Benevolences would have been $136.59 instead of $85.81.

The implications of these differences become clearer when the aggregate totals are calculated by multiplying the theoretical per member giving levels by the number of members reported by these denominations in 1996. Aggregate Total Contributions would then have been $19.2 billion rather than $15.9 billion, a difference of $3.3 billion, or an increase of 21%.

Aggregate Congregational Finances would have been $15.2 billion rather than $13.4 billion, a difference of $1.8 billion, or an increase of 13%.

There would have been a 59% increase in the total amount received for Benevolences. Instead of receiving $2.5 billion in 1996, as these denominations did, they would have received $4.0 billion, a difference of $1.5 billion.

Summary. When per member giving was considered in current dollar values, giving increased each year from 1968 to 1996 to Total Contributions and the subcategory of Congregational Finances. Per member giving also increased to Benevolences in every year except one.

When per member giving was considered in inflation-adjusted 1992 dollars, the majority of the years demonstrated increases to Total Contributions and the two subcategories of Congregational Finances and Benevolences. However, 97% of the increase in Total Contributions was directed to Congregational Finances. Benevolences therefore represented 21% of each church dollar in 1968, and 16% of each church dollar in 1996.

Giving as a percentage of income posted an overall decline between 1968 and 1996 for Total Contributions and the two subcategories of Congregational Finances and Benevolences.

However, while a decline in per member giving as a percentage of income to Congregational Finances was evident between 1968 and 1985, there was an increase during the 1985 to 1996 period. Future data is necessary to determine if the increase noted for 1985-1996 is a sustained reversal of the previous trend of decline. The rate of decline in giving as a percentage of income to Benevolences slowed in the 1985 to 1996 period compared to the 1968 to 1985 period.

From 1995 to 1996, the rate in giving as a percentage of income to Congregational Finances improved. Figures to the second decimal for giving as a percentage of income to Benevolences remained constant from 1995 to 1996, although the unrounded data suggested a slight decline.

The overall decline in giving as a percentage of income from 1968 to 1996 meant that aggregate donations to congregations would have been $3.3 billion more in 1996, had percentage giving levels been at the 1968 levels in 1996.

2

Church Member Giving for 44 Denominations, 1995 to 1996

The 1968-1996 analysis in chapter one considers data for a group of denominations that published their membership and financial information for 1968 and 1985 in the *Yearbook of American and Canadian Churches* (*YACC*) series. That initial set of communions, considered in the first report on which the present series on church giving is based, has served as a denominational composite analyzed for subsequent data years.

Added to the data for 28 of the 29 composite denominations with information for 1996 was data for sixteen additional denominations. These denominations' data for 1995 and 1996 was either published in the relevant editions of the *YACC* series, or obtained directly from denominational offices. By adding the data for these 16 denominations to that of the composite group for these two years, giving patterns in an expanded set of communions can be considered.

In this enlarged comparison, the member sample increased from 29.6 million to 40,410,696 Full or Confirmed Members, and the number of denominations increased from 29 to 44. The larger group of denominations included both The United Methodist Church and The Episcopal Church, which were not included in the original 1968-1985 analysis because of the unavailability of confirmed 1968 data.[6] A list of the denominations included in the present analysis is contained in Appendix A.

Per Member Giving in Inflation-Adjusted 1992 Dollars. As noted in the first chapter of this report, per member giving to Total Contributions increased from 1995 to 1996 for the composite group of 29 denominations in inflation-adjusted 1992 dollars. Specifically, Total Contributions Per Member increased by $14.79 in inflation-adjusted 1992 dollars from 1995 to 1996, from $476.83 in 1995 to $491.62 in 1996. When the group was expanded to 44 denominations, Total Per Member giving increased by $13.72 from 1995 to 1996, from $483.59 in 1995 to $497.31 in 1996.

---

[6]Giving data considered in this analysis was obtained from the *Yearbook of American and Canadian Churches*, except as noted in the appendices.

The composite group of 29 denominations increased per member giving in inflation-adjusted dollars to Congregational Finances by $13.30, from $399.96 in 1995 to $413.25 in 1996. The expanded group increased by $12.51, from $402.75 in 1995 to $415.26 in 1996.

In both groups, giving to Benevolences also increased. In the composite of 29 communions, per member contributions to Benevolences increased from $76.87 to $78.37, an increase of $1.50. There was also an increase in the expanded group of 44 denominations, from $80.84 to $82.05, an increase of $1.21.

Table 7 presents per member giving data for 1995 and 1996 for the expanded group of 44 denominations in inflation-adjusted 1992 dollars, and as a percentage of income. In addition, the change from 1995 to 1996 in per member contributions in inflation-adjusted 1992 dollars, in giving as a percentage of income, and in the percent change in giving as a percentage of income from the 1995 base are also presented in the table.

Table 7:   Per Member Giving in 44 Denominations, 1995 and 1996, in Inflation-Adjusted 1992 Dollars and as a Percentage of Income

Year	Total Contributions Per Member		Congregational Finances		Benevolences	
	$s Given in Inflation-Adj. '92 $	Giving as % of Income	$s Given in Inflation-Adj. '92 $	Giving as % of Income	$s Given in Inflation-Adj. '92 $	Giving as % of Income
1995	$483.59	2.59%	$402.75	2.16%	$80.84	0.43%
1996	$497.31	2.61%	$415.26	2.18%	$82.05	0.43%
Difference from the 1995 Base	$13.72	0.02%	$12.51	0.02%	$1.21	0.00%
% Change in Giving as % of Income from the 1995 Base		0.79%		1.05%		-0.52%

Details in the above table may not compute to the numbers shown due to rounding.

Per Member Giving as a Percentage of Income. In the 1968-1996 composite of 29 denominations, giving as a percentage of income increased to Total Contributions and Congregational Finances, while there was a slight decline in giving to Benevolences from 1995 to 1996. In the composite group of 29 denominations, the percent given to Total Contributions increased from 2.56% in 1995 to 2.58% in 1996. Congregational Finances grew from 2.14% in 1995 to 2.17% in 1996. Benevolences measured 0.41% in 1995 to 0.41% in 1996, although there was a slight decline in the unrounded numbers.

In the expanded group of 44 denominations, giving as a percentage of income also increased to Total Contributions and Congregational Finances. In this expanded set, the percent of income given on a per member basis to Total Contributions grew from 2.59% to 2.61%, and to Congregational Finances, from 2.16% to 2.18%. Again, Benevolences measured the same in both years. In 1995, the figure was 0.43% in 1995, and 0.43% in 1996. As in the case of the 29-denomination composite, a decline was measured in the unrounded figures.

The rate of percent change in giving as a percentage of income for the composite group of 29 denominations was 1.05% from the 1995 base for Total Contributions, compared to 0.79% for the expanded group of 44 denominations. For Congregational Finances, the composite group of 29 denominations had a rate of 1.27% percent change in giving as a percentage of income from the 1995 base, compared to 1.05% for the expanded group of 44 denominations. Benevolences for the composite group of 29 denominations had a -0.08% percent change in giving as a percentage of income from the 1995 base, compared to a rate of -0.52% for the expanded group of 44 denominations.

Summary. When the data set of composite denominations was expanded to include an additional 16 denominations, bringing the total to 44, approximately ten million additional Full or Confirmed Members were added to the data set. In both the composite denominations and the expanded group of 44 denominations, per member giving in inflation-adjusted 1992 dollars increased to Total Contributions, Congregational Finances and Benevolences from 1995-1996. However, the increase in per member contributions to Benevolences was smaller in the expanded group of 44 denominations than in the composite communions.

Giving as a percentage of income increased to Total Contributions and Congregational Finances in both groups of denominations. A decline in giving as a percentage of income to Benevolences was measured, although the rounded percentages indicated the same giving figure for both 1995 and 1996.

3

Church Member Giving in Denominations Defined by Organizational Affiliation, 1968, 1985, and 1996

Although members of evangelical denominations give a higher portion of income than do members of mainline Protestant churches, the rate of decline in giving is faster among the evangelicals than in mainline Protestant denominations.

Also, although giving as a percentage of income improved for mainline Protestant denominations from 1985 to 1996, the entire increase was directed to the category of Congregational Finances. As a result, Benevolences in mainline denominations received less per member in 1996 than in 1968, both in inflation-adjusted dollars and in giving as a percentage of income.

These observations result from a comparison of two subsets of denominations within the larger data set of 29 Protestant communions considered in chapter one of this volume.

In that composite group of 29 denominations, financial data is available for 1968, 1985 and 1996 for eight communions affiliated with the National Association of Evangelicals (NAE).

Seven denominations affiliated with the National Council of the Churches of Christ in the U.S.A. (NCC) also had financial data available for 1968, 1985 and 1996. In the original study that reviewed 1968-1985 data, ten of the denominations included were members of the NCC. Two of these denominations merged in 1987, bringing the number of NCC-affiliated denominations in the larger composite to nine communions. Another denomination in this original grouping indicated it no longer had the staff to compile national financial data after the 1990 data year. That development brought to eight the number of NCC-affiliated denominations with current financial data. This year, one of the eight remaining groups no longer was compiling comprehensive Benevolences data for their communion. A source in that denomination explained that national staff had been downsized, and choices had to be made about which activities to continue. Although this denomination had provided data to the Yearbook of American and Canadian Churches series since 1921, it no longer was continuing to do a survey of its related institutions in 1996. Discussions are underway to recover the data that was not collected that year through the efforts of another affiliated agency. However, the denomination's comprehensive 1996 data was not available when the current report was written.

The giving statistics on the next few pages may help to explain these developments. These numbers indicate that a decrease in giving as a percentage of income is evident across the theological spectrum. Mainline Protestant churches have already been impacted by the decline in giving. Conversations with staff of some evangelical denominations suggest that they may also begin to feel the effects of a downturn in church member giving. An increasing emphasis on congregational activities aggravated a decline in giving to Benevolences, which include denominational support.

The analysis in this chapter considers giving in two segments of the church. Of course, there is diversity of opinion within any denomination, as well as in multi-communion groupings such as the NAE or the NCC. For purposes of the present analysis, however, these two groups may serve as general categories, since they have been characterized as representing certain types of denominations. For example, the National Association of Evangelicals has, by choice of its title, defined its denominational constituency. And traditionally, the National Council of the Churches of Christ in the U.S.A. has counted mainline denominations among its members.

Recognizing that there are limitations in defining a denomination's theological perspectives merely by membership in one of these two organizations, a review of giving patterns of the two subsets of denominations, totaling 15 communions within the larger composite of 29 denominations, may nevertheless provide some insight into how widely spread declining giving patterns may be. Therefore, an analysis of 1968-1996 giving patterns was completed for the two subsets of those denominations which were affiliated with one of these two interdenominational organizations.

Using 1985 data, the eight denominations affiliated with the NAE as of 1996 represented 18% of the total number of NAE-member denominations as listed in the *Yearbook of American and Canadian Churches* (*YACC*) series; 21% of the total number of NAE-member denominations with membership data listed in the *YACC*; and approximately 21% of the total membership of the NAE-member denominations with membership data listed in the *YACC*.[7]

Data for 1996 was also available for seven NCC-member denominations in the larger composite group of 29 denominations. In 1985, these seven denominations represented 24% of the total number of NCC constituent bodies as listed in the *YACC*; 27% of the NCC constituent bodies with membership data listed in the *YACC*; and approximately 29% of the total membership of the NCC constituent bodies with membership data listed in the *YACC*.[8]

---

[7] The 1985 total church membership estimate of 3,388,414 represented by NAE denominations includes *YACC* 1985 membership data for each denomination where available or, if 1985 membership data was not available, membership data for the most recent year prior to 1985. Full or Confirmed membership data was used except in those instances where this figure was not available, in which case Inclusive Membership was used.

[8] The 1985 total church membership estimate of 39,621,950 represented by NCC denominations includes *YACC* 1985 membership data for each denomination where available or, if 1985 membership data was not available, membership data for the most recent year prior to 1985. Full or Confirmed membership data was used except in those instances where this figure was not available, in which case Inclusive Membership was used.

Per Member Giving to Total Contributions, 1968, 1985 and 1996. As noted in Table 8, per member giving as a percentage of income to Total Contributions for a composite of those eight NAE-member denominations was 6.19% in 1968. That year, per member giving as a percentage of income to Total Contributions was 3.32% for a composite of these seven NCC denominations.

Table 8: **Per Member Giving as a Percentage of Income to Total Contributions, Eight NAE and Seven NCC Denominations, 1968, 1985 and 1996**

	Total Contributions									
	NAE Denominations					NCC Denominations				
Year	Number of Denom. Analyzed	Total Contrib. Per Member as % of Income	Diff. in Total Contrib. Per Member as % of Income from Previous Base	Percent Change in Total Contrib. as % of Income Figured from 1968 Base	Avg. Annual Percent Change in Total Contrib. as % of Income	Number of Denom. Analyzed	Total Contrib. Per Member as % of Income	Diff. in Total Contrib. Per Member as % of Income from Previous Base	Percent Change in Total Contrib. as % of Income Figured from 1968 Base	Avg. Annual Percent Change in Total Contrib. as % of Income
1968	8	6.19%				7	3.32%			
1985	8	4.87%	-1.32%	-21.26% from '68	-1.25%	7	2.93%	-0.39%	-11.92% from '68	-0.70%
1996	8	4.10%	-0.77%	-12.48% from '85	-1.13%	7	2.96%	0.03%	0.87% from '85	0.08%

Details in the above table may not compute to the numbers shown due to rounding.

In 1985, the NAE denominations' per member giving as a percentage of income level was 4.87%, while the NCC level was 2.93%.

The data shows the NAE-member denominations received a larger portion of their members' incomes than did NCC-affiliated denominations in both 1968 and 1985. This information supports the assumption that denominations identifying with an evangelical perspective received a higher level of support than denominations that may be termed mainline.

The analysis also indicates that the decline in levels of giving observed in the larger composite of 29 denominations was evident among both the NAE-member denominations and the NCC-member denominations as well. While giving levels decreased for both sets of denominations between 1968 and 1985, the decrease in Total Contributions was more pronounced in the NAE-affiliated communions. The percent change in percentage of income donated in the NAE-member denominations, in comparison to the 1968 base, declined 21% between 1968 and 1985, while the percent change in percentage of income given to the NCC-member denominations declined 12%.

Thus, although the evangelical church members continued to give more than mainline church members, the difference in giving levels was smaller in 1985 than in 1968.

A decline in giving as a percentage of income continued among the eight NAE-member denominations during the 1985-1996 period. By 1996, per member giving as a percentage of income to Total Contributions had declined from the 1985 level of 4.87% to 4.10%, a percentage drop of 12% in the portion of members' incomes donated over that eleven-year period.

Meanwhile, the seven NCC-affiliated denominations increased in giving as a percentage of income to Total Contributions during 1985-1996, from the 1985 level of 2.93% to 2.96% in 1996, a percentage increase of 0.87% in the portion of income given to these churches.

Because of the decline in the portion of income given in the NAE-affiliated denominations, in 1996 the difference in per member giving as a percentage of income between the NAE-affiliated denominations and the NCC-affiliated denominations was not as large as it had been in 1968. Comparing the two rates in giving as a percentage of income to Total Contributions between the NAE-member denominations and the NCC-member denominations in this analysis, the NCC-affiliated denominations received 54% as much of per member income as the NAE-member denominations did in 1968, 60% as much in 1985, and 72% in 1996.

For the NAE-affiliated denominations, during the 1985 to 1996 period, the rate of decrease in the average annual percent change in per member giving as a percentage of income to Total Contributions slowed in comparison to the 1968-1985 annual percent change from the 1968 base. The 1968-1985 average annual percent change was -1.25%. The figure for 1985-1996 was -1.13%.

In the NCC-member denominations, the trend reversed. While the average annual percent change from the 1968 base in giving as a percentage of income was -0.70% between 1968 and 1985, the average annual change from 1985 was an increase of 0.08% between 1985 and 1996.

Per Member Giving to Congregational Finances and Benevolences, 1968, 1985 and 1996. Were there any markedly different patterns between the two subsets of denominations defined by affiliation with the NAE and the NCC in regards to the distribution of Total Contributions between the subcategories of Congregational Finances and Benevolences?

In fact, both subsets of communions displayed the same trend noted in the composite group of 29 denominations. In the overall period of 1968 to 1996, both categories of Congregational Finances and Benevolences declined as a percentage of income in the NCC-affiliated denominations as well as in the NAE-affiliated group. It may be noted, however, that the NCC-related denominations showed an increase in the percentage of income donated to Congregational Finances in the 1985 to 1996 period.

Table 9 presents the Congregational Finances giving data for the NAE and NCC denominations in 1968, 1985 and 1996.

Table 10 presents the Benevolences giving data for the NAE and NCC denominations in 1968, 1985 and 1996.

In 1968, the NAE-affiliated members were giving 6.19% of their incomes to their churches. Of that, 5.04% went to Congregational Finances, while 1.15% went to Benevolences. In 1985, of the 4.87% of income donated to Total Contributions, 3.93% was directed to Congregational Finances. This represented a percent change in the portion of income going to Congregational Finances of -22% from the 1968 base. Per member contributions to

Table 9:   Per Member Giving as a Percentage of Income to Congregational Finances, Eight NAE and Seven NCC Denominations, 1968, 1985 and 1996

	Congregational Finances										
	NAE Denominations						NCC Denominations				
Year	Number of Denom. Analyzed	Cong. Finances Per Member as % of Income	Diff. in Cong. Finances Per Member as % of Income from Previous Base	Percent Change in Cong. Finances as % of Income Figured from 1968 Base	Avg. Annual Percent Change in Cong. Finances as % of Income		Number of Denom. Analyzed	Cong. Finances Per Member as % of Income	Diff. in Cong. Finances Per Member as % of Income from Previous Base	Percent Change in Cong. Finances as % of Income Figured from 1968 Base	Avg. Annual Percent Change in Cong. Finances as % of Income
1968	8	5.04%					7	2.70%			
1985	8	3.93%	-1.11%	-22.05% from '68	-1.30%		7	2.48%	-0.22%	-8.09% from '68	-0.48%
1996	8	3.38%	-0.55%	-10.98% from '85	-1.00%		7	2.59%	0.11%	4.23% from '85	0.38%

Details in the above table may not compute to the numbers shown due to rounding.

Table 10:   Per Member Giving as a Percentage of Income to Benevolences, Eight NAE and Seven NCC Denominations, 1968, 1985 and 1996

	Benevolences										
	NAE Denominations						NCC Denominations				
Year	Number of Denom. Analyzed	Benevol. Per Member as % of Income	Diff. in Benevol. Per Member as % of Income from Previous Base	Percent Change in Benevol. as % of Income Figured from 1968 Base	Avg. Annual Percent Change in Benevol. as % of Income		Number of Denom. Analyzed	Benevol. Per Member as % of Income	Diff. in Benevol. Per Member as % of Income from Previous Base	Percent Change in Benevol. as % of Income Figured from 1968 Base	Avg. Annual Percent Change in Benevol. as % of Income
1968	8	1.15%					7	0.63%			
1985	8	0.94%	-0.21%	-17.76% from '68	-1.04%		7	0.45%	-0.18%	-28.36% from '68	-1.67%
1996	8	0.73%	-0.21%	-19.09% from '85	-1.74%		7	0.37%	-0.08%	-13.54% from '85	-1.23%

Details in the above table may not compute to the numbers shown due to rounding.

Benevolences among these NAE-member denominations declined from 1.15% in 1968 to 0.94% in 1985, representing a percent change of -18% from the 1968 base in the portion of income donated to Benevolences.

In 1996, the 4.10% of income donated by the NAE-member denominations to their churches was divided between Congregational Finances and Benevolences at the 3.38% and 0.73% levels, respectively. The percent change between 1985 and 1996 in contributions to Congregational Finances as a percent of income was a decline of 11%. In contrast, the percent change in contributions to Benevolences as a percent of income was a decline of 19% in the same eleven-year period. The annual rate in the percent change in giving as a percentage of income to Benevolences accelerated to -1.74% between 1985 and 1996, compared to the 1968-1985 rate of -1.04%.

In 1968, the NCC-member denominations were giving 3.32% of their incomes to their churches. Of that, 2.70% went to Congregational Finances. In 1985, of the 2.93% of income donated to these communions, 2.48% went to Congregational Finances. This represented a percent change from the 1968 base in the portion of income going to Congregational Finances of -8%. In contrast, per member contributions as a percent of income to Benevolences among these same NCC-affiliated denominations had declined from 0.63% in 1968 to 0.45% in 1985, representing a percent change of -28% from the 1968 base in the portion of income donated to Benevolences.

In 1996, the 2.96% of income donated by the NCC-affiliated members to their churches was divided between Congregational Finances and Benevolences at the 2.59% and 0.37% levels, respectively. The increase in per member Total Contributions as a percent of income was directed to Congregational Finances, which increased from 2.48% in 1985 to 2.59% in 1996. The 1996 percent change in contributions to Congregational Finances as a percent of income from 1985 was an increase of 4%.

The portion of income directed to Benevolences by these NCC-member denominations declined from 1968 to 1985, and continued to decline from 1985 to 1996. The percent change in contributions to Benevolences as a percent of income declined from 0.45% in 1985 to the 1996 level of 0.37%, a decline of 14% in this eleven-year period. The annual percent change from 1985 in giving as a percentage of income to Benevolences indicated a lower rate of decline at 1.23% between 1985 and 1996, compared to the 1968-1985 annual rate of -1.67%.

Figure 4 presents data for giving as a percentage of income to Total Contributions, Congregational Finances and Benevolences for both the NAE and NCC denominations in graphic form for the years 1968, 1985 and 1996.

Figure 4: **Per Member Giving as a Percentage of Income to Total Contributions, Congregational Finances and Benevolences, Eight NAE and Seven NCC Denominations, 1968, 1985 and 1996**

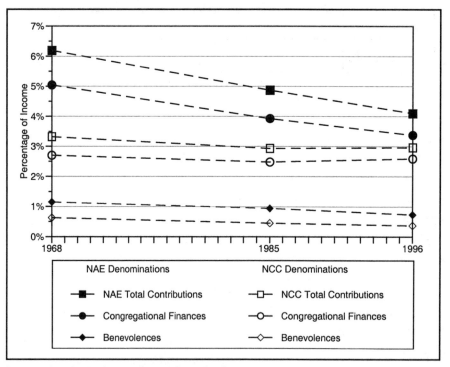

Sources: *Yearbook of American and Canadian Churches,*   empty tomb, inc. 1998
adjusted series; U.S. Bureau of Economic Analysis

Changes in Per Member Giving, 1968 to 1996. For the NAE-affiliated denominations, per member giving as a percentage of income to Congregational Finances declined from 5.04% in 1968 to 3.38% in 1996, a change of -33% from the 1968 base. In Benevolences, the -37% change was due to a decline from 1.15% in 1968 to 0.73% in 1996.

For the NCC-affiliated denominations, between 1968 and 1996, per member giving as a percentage of income declined from 2.70% to 2.59%, a change of -4% in the subcategory of Congregational Finances. That compared to the -42% decline in the subcategory of Benevolences that changed from 0.63% in 1968 to 0.37% in 1996.

Table 11 presents the 1968-1996 percent change in per member giving as a percentage of income to Total Contributions, Congregational Finances and Benevolences in both the NAE- and NCC-affiliated communions.

Table 11: **Percent Change in Per Member Giving as a Percentage of Income, Eight NAE and Seven NCC Denominations, 1968 to 1996**

	NAE Denominations				NCC Denominations			
Year	Number of Denom. Analyzed	Total Contrib.	Cong. Finances	Benevol.	Number of Denom. Analyzed	Total Contrib.	Cong. Finances	Benevol.
1968	8	6.19%	5.04%	1.15%	7	3.32%	2.70%	0.63%
1996	8	4.10%	3.38%	0.73%	7	2.96%	2.59%	0.37%
% Chg. 1968-96	8	-34%	-33%	-37%	7	-11%	-4%	-42%

Per Member Giving in Inflation-Adjusted 1992 Dollars. The NAE-affiliated group level of per member support to Total Contributions in inflation-adjusted 1992 dollars was $693.87 in 1968. This increased to $781.06 in 1985, and declined by 1996 to $780.47.

For the NAE-affiliated denominations, per member contributions in inflation-adjusted 1992 dollars to the subcategory of Congregational Finances increased from 1968 to 1985, and again from 1985 to 1996. Per member contributions in inflation-adjusted 1992 dollars to Benevolences followed the same pattern as Total Contributions, increasing between 1968 and 1985, and decreasing between 1985 and 1996.

The NCC-affiliated group experienced an increase in inflation-adjusted per member Total Contributions between 1968 and 1996. The 1968 NCC level of per member support in inflation-adjusted 1992 dollars was $372.73. In 1985, this had increased to $469.31, and in 1996 the figure was $562.83.

The NCC-member denominations experienced an increase in inflation-adjusted per member donations to Congregational Finances in both 1985 and 1996 as well. However, while gifts to Benevolences increased between 1968 and 1985 in inflation-adjusted 1992 dollars, the level of per member contributions to Benevolences decreased between 1985 and 1996.

As a portion of Total Contributions, the NAE-member denominations directed 19% of their per member gifts to Benevolences in 1968, 19% in 1985, and 18% in 1996. The NCC-member denominations directed 19% of their per member gifts to Benevolences in 1968, 15% in 1985, and 12% in 1996.

Table 12 below presents the levels of per member giving to Total Contributions, Congregational Finances and Benevolences, in inflation-adjusted 1992 dollars, and the percentage of Total Contributions which went to Benevolences in 1968, 1985 and 1996, for both sets of denominations. In addition, the percent change from 1968 to 1996, from the 1968 base, in per member inflation-adjusted 1992 dollar contributions is noted.

Table 12: Per Member Giving, Eight NAE and Seven NCC Denominations, 1968, 1985 and 1996, Inflation-Adjusted 1992 Dollars

	NAE Denominations					NCC Denominations				
Year	Number of Denom. Analyzed	Total Contrib.	Cong. Finances	Benevol.	Benevol. as % of Total Contrib.	Number of Denom. Analyzed	Total Contrib.	Cong. Finances	Benevol.	Benevol. as % of Total Contrib.
1968	8	$693.87	$565.14	$128.73	19%	7	$372.73	$302.25	$70.48	19%
1985	8	$781.06	$629.72	$151.34	19%	7	$469.31	$397.13	$72.18	15%
1996	8	$780.47	$642.47	$138.00	18%	7	$562.83	$493.32	$69.51	12%
$ Diff. '68-'96		$86.60	$77.33	$9.27			$190.11	$191.07	-$0.96	
% Chg. '68-'96		12.5%	13.7%	7.2%			51.0%	63.2%	-1.4%	

Details in the above table may not compute to the numbers shown due to rounding.

Figure 5 presents the data for per member contributions in inflation-adjusted 1992 dollars in graphic form for the years 1968, 1985 and 1996.

Aggregate Dollar Donations, 1968 and 1996. In terms of per member inflation-adjusted 1992 dollar gifts among the NCC-member churches during the 1968-1996 period, the data indicates an increase to Total Contributions and Congregational Finances, but a decline in per member gifts to Benevolences. The NAE-member denominations posted increases in all three categories, including Benevolences.

However, a decrease from 1968 to 1996 in per member giving as a percentage of income to all categories among the NAE-member and NCC-member denominations in this analysis suggests that the decline in giving patterns among church members is evident across the theological spectrum. Whatever factors are contributing to this decline, they are not limited to one specific part of the church.

One distinguishing difference between the two subsets of communions was the growth in membership that the evangelical denominations experienced during this period, in contrast to the membership decline reported by the mainline denominations.

While both decreased in per member giving to Benevolences as a percentage of income, the NAE-member denominations grew in membership, and the NCC-member denominations declined in membership. In the NAE-affiliated communions, while members were giving a smaller percentage of income to Benevolences in 1996 than in 1968, the aggregate total dollars available increased. For the NCC-affiliated communions, a decline in per member giving as a percentage of income, as well as in inflation-adjusted 1992 dollars

Figure 5: **Per Member Giving to Total Contributions, Congregational Finances and Benevolences, Eight NAE and Seven NCC Member Denominations, 1968, 1985 and 1996, Inflation-Adjusted 1992 Dollars**

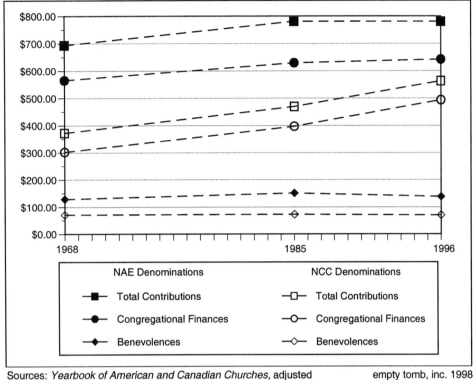

Sources: *Yearbook of American and Canadian Churches,* adjusted series; U.S. Bureau of Economic Analysis

empty tomb, inc. 1998

to Benevolences, was coupled with a decrease in membership. Thus, for the NCC-affiliated communions, there was a decrease in aggregate inflation-adjusted Benevolences between 1968 and 1996.

Table 13 considers aggregate giving data for the eight NAE-member denominations included in this study for which data was available for both 1968 and 1996. Membership in these eight NAE-member denominations increased 54% from 1968-1996. Even though per member giving as a percentage of income declined to Total Contributions and the two subcategories of Congregation Finances and Benevolences for the NAE-affiliated denominations, per member giving in inflation-adjusted dollars increased in each of the three categories from 1968 to 1996.

Table 13: **Aggregate Giving, Eight NAE Denominations, 1968 and 1996, in Current and Inflation-Adjusted 1992 Dollars**

			Current Dollars			Inflation-Adjusted 1992 Dollars		
Year	Number of Den. Analyzed	Member-ship	Total Contributions	Cong. Finances	Benevol.	Total Contributions	Cong. Finances	Benevol.
1968	8	535,865	$102,845,802	$83,765,677	$19,080,125	$371,821,410	$302,840,481	$68,980,929
1996	8	824,168	$704,346,294	$579,810,399	$124,535,895	$643,238,625	$529,507,214	$113,731,411
% Chg.		54%	585%	592%	553%	73%	75%	65%

Details in the above table may not compute to the numbers shown due to rounding.

As measured in current dollars, giving in each of the three categories of Total Contributions, Congregational Finances and Benevolences was greater in 1996 than in 1968 for the NAE-member denominations.

The same can be said for the three aggregate categories when inflation was factored out by converting the current dollars to inflation-adjusted 1992 dollars. These denominations have been compensated for a decline in giving as a percentage of income by the increase in total membership. As long as these denominations continue to grow in membership and maintain constant levels of giving, their national and regional programs may not be affected in the immediate future in the same way some of the mainline Protestant communions have been impacted by a combination of declining giving and membership.

Table 14 below considers aggregate data for the seven NCC-member denominations. The NCC-related denominations also experienced an increase in aggregate current dollars in each of the three categories of Total Contributions, Congregational Finances and Benevolences, even with a posted decline in membership.

However, the inflation-adjusted 1992 dollar figures account for the acknowledged financial difficulties in many of these communions, particularly in the category of Benevolences. The decline in membership affected the total income received by this group of denominations. Between 1968 and 1996, while the NCC-related communions experienced an increase of 51% in per member giving to Total Contributions in inflation-adjusted 1992 dollars—from $372.73 in 1968 to $562.83 in 1996—aggregate Total Contributions in 1996 to these eight denominations was only 12% larger in inflation-adjusted 1992 dollars in 1996 than in 1968.

In regard to the two categories of Congregational Finances and Benevolences, Congregational Finances absorbed the increased giving. The -27% decline in aggregated Benevolences receipts in inflation-adjusted 1992 dollars between 1968 and 1996 provides insight into the basis for any cutbacks at the denominational level.

Table 14:   Aggregate Giving, Seven NCC Denominations, 1968 and 1996, in Current and Inflation-Adjusted 1992 Dollars

Year	Number of Den. Analyzed	Member-ship	Current Dollars			Inflation-Adjusted 1992 Dollars		
			Total Contributions	Cong. Finances	Benevol.	Total Contributions	Cong. Finances	Benevol.
1968	7	12,688,864	$1,308,180,158	$1,060,822,881	$247,357,277	$4,729,501,656	$3,835,223,720	$894,277,936
1996	7	9,382,757	$5,782,629,780	$5,068,435,698	$714,194,082	$5,280,940,438	$4,628,708,400	$652,232,038
% Chg.		-26%	342%	378%	189%	12%	21%	-27%

Details in the above table may not compute to the numbers shown due to rounding.

Summary. An analysis of giving as a percentage of income found a negative trend between 1968 and 1996 in the portion of income given by church members across the theological spectrum. Denominations affiliated with both the NAE and the NCC were receiving a lower level of giving as a percentage of income on a per member basis.

On one hand, the NAE-member denominations received a higher portion of income on a per member basis than did the NCC-member denominations throughout this period. On the other hand, between 1968 and 1985, the NAE-member denominations experienced a higher rate of decrease in average annual percent change in giving as a percentage of income, from the 1968 base, in the categories of Total Contributions and Congregational Finances than did the NCC-member denominations. In the category of Benevolences, between 1968 and 1985, the NCC-member denominations had a higher rate of decrease in average annual percent change in giving as a percentage of income from the 1968 base than did the NAE-member denominations.

Between 1985 and 1996, the NAE-member denominations experienced a higher rate of decrease in average annual percent change in per member giving as a percentage of income from the 1985 base than did the NCC-member denominations in each of the three categories of Total Contributions, Congregational Finances and Benevolences. Further, in the category of Congregational Finances, the NCC-member denominations increased from 1985 to 1996.

In the NAE-member denominations, the rate of decrease in per member giving as a percentage of income to Benevolences quickened during the 1985-1996 period compared to the 1968-1985 period. In the NCC-member denominations, the rate of decrease in per member giving as a percentage of income to Benevolences slowed between 1985-1996, compared to 1968-1985.

After inflation was factored out by converting the data to inflation-adjusted 1992 dollars, both the NAE-affiliated and the NCC-affiliated denominations received more dollars per member for the categories of Total Contributions and Congregational Finances in 1996 than in 1968. In the Benevolences category, the NAE-affiliated denominations also received more per member in inflation-adjusted 1992 dollars. The NCC-affiliated denominations received less per member for Benevolences in inflation-adjusted 1992 dollars.

The NAE-affiliated denominations were growing in membership during the 1968-1996 period. As a result, aggregate income to these denominations also increased. In the NCC-affiliated denominations, a decline in per member giving in inflation-adjusted 1992 dollars to Benevolences coincided with a decline in membership. The result was a decrease in aggregate Benevolences for the NCC-member denominations between 1968 and 1996 in inflation-adjusted dollars.

The generally-held belief that evangelicals were "better givers" than mainline members is correct in that per member giving was higher in the NAE-affiliated denominations both in terms of giving as a percentage of income and inflation-adjusted contributions when compared to NCC-member denominations throughout the 1968 to 1996 period.

However, the rate of decline in per member giving as a percentage of income between 1985 and 1996 was more pronounced among the NAE-affiliated denominations than among the NCC-affiliated denominations for the categories of Total Contributions and Congregational Finances. The rate of decline in the NCC-affiliated denominations was greater than that of the NAE-affiliated denominations for the category of Benevolences.

The negative direction in per member giving as a percentage of income over the 29-year time span under review in both the NAE-affiliated and NCC-affiliated denominations suggests that the negative trend in giving patterns is not limited to a particular portion of the theological spectrum.

4

Church Member Giving in Eleven Denominations, 1921-1996_____

A continuing feature in this ongoing series reviewing church member giving is an analysis of available giving data throughout this century. Because of the fixed nature of the data source, the analysis remains fairly static. However, recent income series revisions by the United States Bureau of Economic Analysis has had some impact on the more recent years in this century-long overview. Also, the data can now be updated to include information through 1996. For these reasons, and for the benefit of readers who may be new to this series this year, the analysis is presented once again in this chapter, updated through 1996.

The preferable approach would be to analyze the entire data set of 29 denominations considered in chapter one of this volume for the period 1921 through 1996. Unfortunately, comparable data since 1921 is not readily available for all 29 communions in the composite analysis. However, data over an extended period of time is available in the Yearbook of *American and Canadian Churches* series for a group of 11 Protestant communions, or their historical antecedents. This set includes ten mainline Protestant communions and the Southern Baptist Convention.

The available data has been reported fairly consistently over the time span of 1921 to 1996.[9] The value of the multiyear comparison is that it provides a historical time line over which to observe giving patterns.

Giving as a Percentage of Income. The period under consideration in this section of the report began in 1921. At that point, per member giving as a percentage of income was 2.9%. In current dollars, U.S. per capita disposable (after-tax) personal income was $555, and per member giving was $16. When inflation was factored out by converting both income and giving to 1992 dollars, per capita income in 1921 measured $4,479 and per member giving was $130.

---

[9] Data for the period 1965-1967 was not available in a form that could be readily analyzed for the present purposes, and therefore data for these three years was estimated by dividing the change in per member current dollar contributions from 1964 to 1968 by four, the number of years in this interval, and cumulatively adding the result to the base year of 1964 data and subsequently to the calculated data for the succeeding years of 1965 and 1966 in order to obtain estimates for the years 1965-1967.

From 1922 through 1933, giving as a percent of income stayed above the 3% level. The high was 3.68% in 1924, followed closely by the amount in 1932, when per member giving measured 3.65% of per capita income. This trend is of particular interest inasmuch as per capita income was increasing steadily between 1921 and 1927, with the exception of a decline in 1925. Even as people were increasing in personal affluence, they also continued to maintain a giving level of more than 3% to their churches. Even after income began to decline because of the economic reverses in the Great Depression, giving measured above 3% from 1929 through 1933.

The year 1933 was the depth of the Great Depression. Per capita income was at the lowest point it would reach between 1921 and 1996, whether measured in current or inflation-adjusted dollars. Yet per member giving as a percentage of income was 3.3%. Income had decreased by 17% between 1921 and 1933 in inflation-adjusted 1992 dollars, from $4,479 to $3,727. Meanwhile, per member giving had decreased 6%, from $130 in 1921 to $123 in 1933, in inflation-adjusted dollars. Therefore, giving as a percentage of income actually increased from 2.9% in 1921 to 3.3% in 1933, an increase of 13% in the portion of income contributed to the church.

Giving in inflation-adjusted 1992 dollars declined from 1933 to 1934, although income began to recover in 1934. Giving then began to increase again in 1935. In inflation-adjusted dollars, giving did not recover to the 1927 level of $200 until 1953, when giving grew from $192 in 1952 to $211 in 1953.

During World War II, incomes improved rapidly. Meanwhile, church member giving increased only modestly in current dollars. When inflation was factored out, per member giving was at $126.61 in 1941, the year the United States entered the war. It declined to $123.24 in 1942, increased in 1943 to $124.73, and then to $136.98 in 1944. However, income in inflation-adjusted dollars grew from $6,061 in 1941 to $7,061 in 1942, $7,542 in 1943, and reached a high for this period of $7,949 in 1944, a level that would not be surpassed again until 1953. Thus, giving as a percentage of income reached a low point of 1.7% during 1942, 1943 and 1944, the three full calendar years of formal U.S. involvement in World War II.

In 1945, the last year of the war, U.S. per capita income was $7,850 in inflation-adjusted dollars. Giving in inflation-adjusted dollars was $155 that year. Although per member giving increased 26% between 1933 and 1945, per capita income had increased 111%. Giving as a percentage of income therefore declined from the 3.3% level in 1933, to 2.0% in 1945.

The unusually high level of per capita income slumped after the war but had recovered to war levels by the early 1950s. By 1960, U.S. per capita income was 10% higher in inflation-adjusted 1992 dollars than it had been in 1945, increasing from $7,850 in 1945 to $8,647 in 1960. Meanwhile, per member giving in inflation-adjusted dollars had increased 75%, from $155 in 1945 to $272 in 1960. Giving recovered the level it had been from 1922 through 1933, and stayed above 3% from 1958 through 1963. Giving as a percentage of income reached a postwar high of 3.15% in 1960, and then began to decline.

In contrast to the earlier years in the century, when incomes were interrupted by the Great Depression, the economy continued to expand through the 1960s. Yet the level of giving as a portion of income was not sustained. By 1968, giving as a percentage of income had declined to 2.7% for this group of 11 communions. U.S. per capita income increased 30% in inflation-adjusted 1992 dollars between 1960 and 1968, from $8,647 in 1960 to $11,211 in 1968. In comparison, per member giving had increased 10% in inflation-adjusted dollars, from the 1960 level of $272 to the 1968 level of $298.

By 1985, per member giving had increased 32% in inflation-adjusted 1992 dollars, from $298 in 1968 to $393 in 1985. U.S. per capita income measured $16,026, an increase of 43% over the 1968 level of $11,211. Giving as a percentage of income measured 2.45% in 1985.

The year 1996 was the latest year for which data was available for the eleven denominations considered in this section. In that year, per member giving as a percentage of income was 2.47%, an increase from the 1985 level of 2.45%. Per member giving had increased 20% in inflation-adjusted 1992 dollars, from $393 in 1985 to $471 in 1996. U.S. per capita income had increased 19% during this period, from the 1985 level of $16,026 to the 1996 level of $19,032. Thus, the percentage of income donated increased slightly.

Figure 6 contrasts per member giving as a percentage of income for a composite of eleven Protestant denominations, with U.S. disposable personal income in inflation-adjusted 1992 dollars, for the period 1921 through 1996.

Figure 6: **Per Member Giving as a Percentage of Income in 11 Denominations, and U.S. Per Capita Income, 1921-1996**

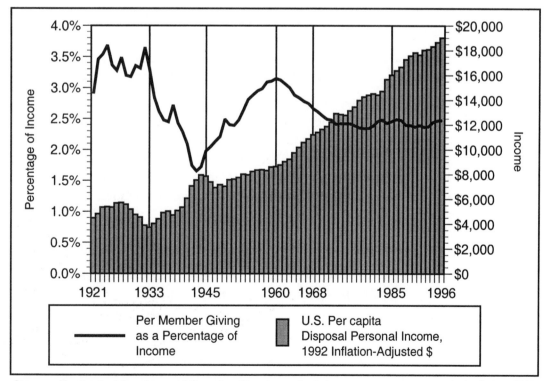

Sources: *Yearbook of American and Canadian Churches,* adjusted series; U.S. Bureau of Economic Analysis

empty tomb, inc. 1998

Change in Per Member Giving and U.S. Per Capita Disposable Personal Income, in Inflation-adjusted 1992 Dollars. For this group of 11 communions, per member giving in inflation-adjusted 1992 dollars increased in the majority of years during the 1921-1947 period. Per member giving in inflation-adjusted dollars decreased from 1924 to 1925. While it increased from 1925 to 1926 and again in 1927, giving began a seven-year decline in 1928. This seven-year period, from 1928 to 1934, included some of the worst years of the Great Depression. Giving increased again in 1935. Declines in 1939, 1940, 1942, 1946 and 1947 alternated with increases in the other years.

Then, from 1947 through 1968,[10] these 11 communions experienced uninterrupted increases in per member giving in inflation-adjusted 1992 dollars for 21 years in a row. Further, the period from 1947 to the year 1960, when giving as a percentage of income reached its postwar peak, posted the highest prolonged annual increase in per member giving in inflation-adjusted dollars during this 1921-1996 period of 76 years. During the 1947-1960 interval of 13 years, per member giving averaged an increase of $9.57 a year. Although giving continued to increase for the next few years from 1960 to 1968, it was at the slower rate of $3.26 per year.

Per member giving in inflation-adjusted dollars declined annually from 1968 through 1971, followed by two years of increase and two of decline.

There was also a sustained increase during the 21-year interval of 1975-1996. During this interval, income increased an average of $297.56 annually in inflation-adjusted 1992 dollars. Meanwhile, per member giving increased $7.68 on average each year, a higher rate than during the 21-year interval of 1947-1968, when the annual increase was $7.16. Overall, giving increased 49% from 1975 to 1996, while income increased 46%. Therefore, giving as a percentage of income was 2.42% in 1975 and 2.47% in 1996.

By reviewing this data in smaller increments of years from 1950 to 1996, as presented in Table 15, the time period in which giving began to decline markedly can be identified.

As indicated in Table 15, the period 1950 to 1955 was the period of highest annual increase in per member giving in inflation-adjusted 1992 dollars. In terms of the highest annual increase in giving as a percentage of the annual change in U.S. per capita income, that period was the years 1955 to 1960. The period 1980 to 1985 produced a higher average per member annual dollar increase of $11.07 than the $6.91 given in 1955-1960. However, the larger amount of $11.07 represented only 3.42% of the average annual increase in U.S. per capita income, compared to the 8.51% which the $6.91 increase in giving represented from 1955 to 1960. The smaller annual increase in dollars given of $8.07 in the 1990-1996 period also represented a higher portion of the average annual increase in income than that of the 1980-1985 period.

Giving declined markedly between 1960 and 1964 in these communions.[11] While income was increasing at an annual rate of $277 in this four-year period, 241% greater than

---

[10] Excluding the years 1965 through 1967 for which estimated data is used. See first footnote in this chapter.

[11] See the first footnote in this chapter for an explanation of the selection of 1960-1964 and 1964-1970, rather than 1960-1965 and 1965-1970

Table 15: **Average Annual Increase in U.S. Per Capita Income and Per Member Giving in 11 Denominations, 1950-1996, Inflation-adjusted 1992 Dollars**

Time Period	U.S. Per Capita Income			Per Member Giving			Avg. Ann. Chg. Giv. as % Avg. Ann. Chg. Income
	First Year in Period	Last Year in Period	Average Annual Change	First Year in Period	Last Year in Period	Average Annual Change	
1950-1955	$7,556	$8,241	$136.98	$181.36	$237.61	$11.25	8.21%
1955-1960	$8,241	$8,647	$81.19	$237.61	$272.14	$6.91	8.51%
1960-1964[12]	$8,647	$9,755	$277.02	$272.14	$281.30	$2.29	0.83%
1964-1970[12]	$9,755	$11,639	$314.06	$281.00	$296.61	$2.55	0.81%
1970-1975	$11,639	$12,783	$228.77	$296.61	$309.32	$2.54	1.11%
1975-1980	$12,783	$14,409	$325.07	$309.32	$337.96	$5.73	1.76%
1980-1985	$14,409	$16,026	$323.58	$337.96	$393.31	$11.07	3.42%
1985-1990	$16,026	$17,824	$359.59	$393.31	$422.13	$5.76	1.60%
1990-1996	$17,824	$19,032	$201.26	$422.13	$470.53	$8.07	4.01%

Details in the above table may not compute to the numbers shown due to rounding.

in the 1955-1960 period, the average annual increase in per member contributions in inflation-adjusted 1992 dollars was $2.29, 67% smaller in 1960-1964 than it was in 1955-1960.

The 1960-1964 period predates many of the controversial issues often cited as reasons for declining giving. Also, it was at the end of the 1960-1964 period when membership began to decrease in mainline denominations, ten of which are included in this group. Therefore, additional exploration of that period of time might be merited.

Increases in per member giving were consistently low from 1960-1975. The annual rates of increase of $2.29 per year from 1960 to 1964, $2.55 from 1964 to 1970, and $2.54 from 1970 to 1975, were the lowest in the 1950 to 1996 period. Throughout the 1960 to 1970 period, the increase in dollars given represented less than one percent of the average annual increase in per capita income, while from 1970-1975, it was 1.11%.

In the 1975-1980 period, the average annual increase in giving increased to $5.73, representing 1.76% of the average annual increase in per capita income.

From 1980 to 1985, the average annual increase in giving rose to $11.07. This amount of $11.07—representing 3.42% of the average annual increase in income during the 1980-1985 period—was the second highest average annual rate of increase in terms of per member giving in inflation-adjusted dollars during the 1950 to 1996 period. As a portion of the increase in per capita income, the 3.42% of the 1980 to 1985 period was the fourth largest annual rate of increase in the 1950 to 1996 period.

The annual average increase in giving as a percent of the average annual income increase from 1985 to 1990 fell from the 1980 to 1985 period. The average annual rate of change increased in the six-year period from 1990 to 1996. The rate increased both in terms of change in per member giving in inflation-adjusted dollars, and as a percent of the average annual income increase.

---

[12] See the first footnote in this chapter for an explanation of the selection of 1960-1964 and 1964-1970, rather than 1960-1965 and 1965-1970

Per Member Giving as Percentage of Income, 1921, 1933 and 1996. By 1996, U.S. per capita disposable (after-tax) personal income had increased 325%, in inflation-adjusted 1992 dollars, since 1921, and 411% since 1933—the depth of the Great Depression.

Meanwhile, by 1996, per member giving in inflation-adjusted 1992 dollars had increased 325% since 1921, and 411% since the depth of the Great Depression.

Consequently, per member giving as a percentage of income was lower in 1996 than in either 1921 or 1933. In 1921, per member giving as a percentage of income was 2.9%. In 1933, it was 3.3%. In 1996, per member giving as a percentage of income was 2.5% for the composite of the eleven denominations considered in this section. Thus, the percent change in the per member portion of income donated to the church had declined by 15% from the 1921 base, from 2.9% in 1921 to 2.5% in 1996, and by 25% from the 1933 base, from 3.3% in 1933 to 2.5% in 1996.

Appendix A contains a listing of the denominations contained in this analysis.

Summary. For a group of 11 Protestant denominations, giving as a percentage of income was above 3% of U.S. per capita disposable personal income from 1922 through 1933. It dropped below 3% in the later part of the Great Depression and reached a low point during World War II. The level of giving improved until, from 1958 through 1963, it recovered, reaching the levels evident earlier in the century, maintaining at more than 3%. The post-war high was reached in 1960, after which giving began to decline as a portion of income.

During the years 1921-1996, two 21-year periods posted increases in per member giving in inflation-adjusted 1992 dollars. Per member giving during the years 1947 to 1968 increased by an annual average of $7.16. During 1975-1996, the annual average increase was $7.68.

Per member giving and U.S. per capita disposable personal income, both in inflation-adjusted 1992 dollars, were analyzed in four, five or six-year increments for the years 1950-1996. The data indicates there was a marked decline in the rate of giving increase in the 1960-1964 period.

The data also indicates that giving as a portion of income was higher in both 1921 and 1933 than in 1996.

5

Church Member Giving and Membership Trends Based on 1968-1996 Data

As the millennium approaches, more people are imagining what the future might look like. Corporations are hiring professional "futurists" to pinpoint trends that will make the businesses leaders in the next century. The public is buying books on how to cope with the trends that businesses are trying to identify.

Governments and social scientists also use projections to help prepare for the future soon to be here.

The Japanese government, for example, is facing a challenge as early as the next century. The low birth rate in that country may so deplete the work force that there will be little base to support the pensions and health care costs that may quadruple by the year 2025. The national Health Ministry underscored the issue by releasing a projection suggesting current birth trends mean the Japanese people will no longer exist by the year 3500. The government is now exploring incentives to encourage couples to have children.[13]

In the United States, the impact of welfare reform on the health of children has been a particular concern in some quarters. The number of children not covered by health insurance may accelerate, some leaders fear. "While we can't predict actual numbers, we can quantify a steady decline," the executive vice president of the non-partisan Alliance for Health Reform announced. The goal is to use the data to develop policies in the present to prevent what could be a destructive situation for individuals and society in the future.[14]

Statistical analyses help concerned leaders address issues that will affect the quality of life for future generations 25 or 100 years from now. Such projections can be used to identify policy concerns, as in the case of Japanese population demographics. Projections can also encourage changes in present behaviors to produce an alternative outcome than the one now raising concern, such as child welfare in the United States.

---

[13]Joseph Coleman, an Associated Press article appearing as "Japan Confronts a Childless Future" in *Champaign (Ill.) News-Gazette*, August 2, 1998, B-1, col. 1-5.
[14]"More kids lack health coverage," a Knight-Ridder article appearing in *Champaign (Ill.) News-Gazette*, August 17, 1996, C-5, col. 3-6.

Statistical techniques can also be used to suggest both consequences and possibilities regarding church giving and membership patterns as well. This type of trend analysis is useful in considering what data suggests the future will look like if the patterns of the past three decades continue in an uninterrupted fashion.

The Meaning of Trends. Linear regression and exponential regression are both standard statistical techniques that can be used to provide trend projections. The results of such analyses should be evaluated with the realization that these types of projections indicate—rather than dictate—future directions. For example, in the present church member giving analysis, the data can be used to develop giving trends that suggest what giving will look like in coming decades. These trends indicate the present general direction of giving. Various factors—such as intentional education efforts by congregations and/or denominations, or spiritual renewal, or a decided loss of commitment to the church—could change giving patterns in unforeseen ways, either positively or negatively. Trends, therefore, are based on the assumption that either current conditions will remain constant, or present suppositions regarding the future are valid. The trends point out the future of giving, if patterns continue without interruption. With those considerations in mind, one may explore what implications present data patterns have for the future.

This analysis was first conducted, in part, as a result of present church conditions. After talking with numerous denominational officials who were making painful decisions about which programs to cut, in light of decreased Benevolences dollars being received, it seemed useful to see where the present patterns of giving might lead if effective means were not found to alter present behavior. Were current patterns likely to prove a temporary setback, or did the data suggest longer-term implications?

The Current Trend in Church Giving. The first chapter in this report indicates that per member giving as a percentage of income has been decreasing over a 29-year period. Further, contributions to the category of Benevolences have been declining proportionately faster than those to Congregational Finances between 1968 and 1996.

The data for the composite denominations analyzed for 1968 through 1996 has been projected in *The State of Church Giving* series, beginning with the edition that included 1991 data.[15] The most recent projection is based on data from 1968 through 1996.

The data for both Benevolences and Congregational Finances can be projected using linear and exponential regression analysis. To determine which type of analysis more accurately describes the data in a category's giving patterns, the data for 1968-1985 was projected using both techniques. Then, the actual data for 1986 through 1996 was plotted. The more accurate projection was judged to be the procedure that produced the trend line most closely resembling the actual 1986-1996 data.

The Trend in Benevolences. Of the two subcategories within Total Contributions, that is, Congregational Finances and Benevolences, the more pronounced negative trend

---

[15]John Ronsvalle and Sylvia Ronsvalle, *The State of Church Giving through 1991* (Champaign, IL: empty tomb, inc., 1993), and subsequent editions in the series. The edition with data through 1991 provides a discussion of the choice to use giving as a percentage of income as a basis for considering future giving patterns.

occurred in Benevolences. Between 1968 and 1996, per member contributions to Benevolences as a percentage of income decreased from 0.66% in 1968 to 0.41% in 1996, a percent change in giving as a percentage of income of -37% from the 1968 base. In contrast, the percent change in giving as a percentage of income to Congregational Finances declined 12% from the 1968 base, from 2.46% in 1968 to 2.17% in 1996.

The data for giving as a percentage of income to Benevolences for the 17-year interval of 1968 through 1985 was projected using both linear and exponential regression. The actual data for 1986 through 1996 was also included. The results are shown in Figure 7.

Figure 7:   Trend in Giving as a Percentage of Income to Benevolences, Composite Denominations, Linear and Exponential Regression Based on Data for 1968-1985, with Actual Data for 1986-1996

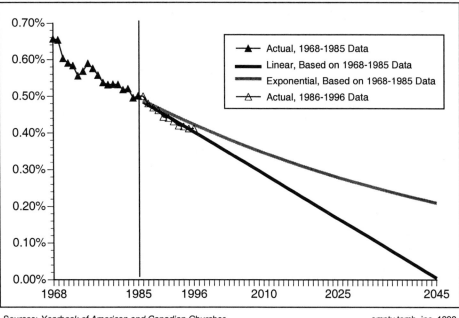

Sources: *Yearbook of American and Canadian Churches,* adjusted series; U.S. Bureau of Economic Analysis

empty tomb, inc. 1998

Both the linear and exponential trends corresponded closely to the actual data for giving as a percentage of income to Benevolences for 1986 to 1996. Per member giving as a percentage of income to Benevolences measured below the linear trends in the five years from 1990 through 1994. However, there was an upturn during 1995 and 1996. As a result, only future data will indicate which trend best describes long-term giving to Benevolences.

In the meantime, a range of giving levels can be offered. If the giving patterns of the past 29 years continue in an uninterrupted fashion, then per member giving as a portion of income to the category of Benevolences will reach 0% of income in the year A.D. 2046, if the linear trend is more accurate, or .21% if the exponential curve proves to be more descriptive.[16] These levels compare to the 0.66% level in 1968, and 0.41% in 1996. In the year 2046, the amount of income going to support Benevolences, including denominational structures, would be either negligible or severely reduced if current patterns hold constant.

The Trend in Congregational Finances. The church giving data contained in this report indicated that, while there was a less pronounced trend in Congregational Finances, giving as a percentage of income also declined between 1968 and 1996 to that category.

Once again, both linear and exponential regression were used to analyze the data for giving as a percentage of income to Congregational Finances for the 17-year interval of 1968 through 1985. The actual data for 1986 through 1996 was also included. The results are shown in Figure 8.

Figure 8:   Trend in Giving as a Percentage of Income to Congregational Finances, Composite Denominations, Linear and Exponential Regression Based on Data for 1968-1985, with Actual Data for 1986-1996

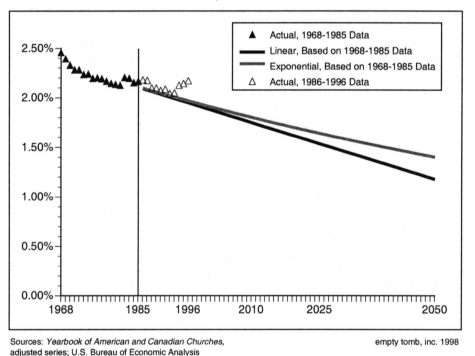

Sources: *Yearbook of American and Canadian Churches,* adjusted series; U.S. Bureau of Economic Analysis

empty tomb, inc. 1998

---

[16]In the linear regression, the value for the correlation coefficient, or r_{XY}, for the Benevolences data is -.98. The strength of the linear relationship in the present set of 1968-1996 data, that is, the proportion of variance accounted for by linear regression, is represented by the coefficient of determination, or r^2_{XY}, of .96 for Benevolences. In the exponential regression, the value for the r_{XY} for the Benevolences data is also -.98, while the strength of the exponential relationship is .97, which is slightly higher than the linear regression. The Benevolences F-observed values of 733.35 for the linear, and 844.40 for the curvilinear, regression are substantially greater than the F-critical value of 7.68 for 1 and 27 degrees of freedom for a single-tailed test with an Alpha value of 0.01. Therefore, the regression equation is useful at the level suggested by the r^2_{XY} figure in predicting giving as a percentage of income.

In the case of giving as a percentage of income to Congregational Finances, the actual data for 1986-1996 was at or above the exponential curve in contrast to the linear regression line. That data suggests that by the year 2050, a few years after Benevolences may represent as low as 0% of members' incomes, giving to Congregational Finances will be at 1.40%, down from 2.17% in 1996, a decrease of 35% in the portion of income donated to support the activities of the congregations.

Membership in the Composite Denominations, 1968-1996. Earlier chapters discuss the patterns in church member giving in a data set for a composite of denominations. How does membership for this group of denominations fare in addition to giving patterns?

Figure 9 presents 1968-1996 per member giving as a percentage of income, as well as membership as a percentage of U.S. population for the composite denominations. This group of denominations which span the theological spectrum included 28,219,613 Full or Confirmed Members in 1968. By 1996, these communions included 30,604,527 members, an increase of 8%.[17] However, during the same 29-year period, U.S. population had

Figure 9: **Giving as a Percentage of Income and Membership as a Percentage of U.S. Population, Composite Denominations, 1968-1996**

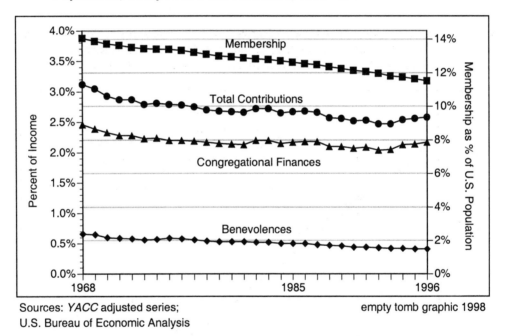

Sources: *YACC* adjusted series;   empty tomb graphic 1998
U.S. Bureau of Economic Analysis

---

[17]Of the 30 denominations in the composite data set considered in earlier chapters, financial information was not available for the Friends United Meeting after 1990. Therefore, the composite was referred to as a set of 29 denominations. This was true even though the Church of the Brethren, one of the 29, did not provide complete 1996 financial data in time for the current report. As of this edition, inclusive membership for the Friends United Meeting was obtained for 1991 through 1996. Therefore, in this chapter, the composite set of denominations generally refers to a set of 29 denominations regarding financial data (actually 28 for 1996), and 30 denominations for membership analysis. See Appendix B-1 for details. Consult Appendix B-4 for the Full or Confirmed Membership numbers used for the American Baptist Churches in the U.S.A. See Appendix B-3.3 and Appendix B-4 for the membership data of the other denominations included in subsequent analyses in this chapter that are not one of the composite denominations.

increased from 200,745,000 to 265,579,000, an increase of 32%. Therefore, while this grouping represented 14% of the U.S. population in 1968, it included 12% in 1996.

Trends in Church Membership as a Percentage of U.S. Population.[18] *The State of Church Giving through 1993* includes a chapter entitled, "A Unified Theory of Giving and Membership." The hypothesis explored in that discussion is that there is a relationship between a decline in church member giving and membership patterns. One proposal considered in that chapter is that a denomination which is able to involve its members in a larger vision as evidenced in giving patterns will also be attracting additional members.

In the present edition, discussion will be limited to patterns and trends in membership as a percentage of U.S. population.

Membership in Ten Mainline Denominations. The declining membership trends have been noticed most markedly in the mainline Protestant communions. Full or Confirmed Membership in ten mainline Protestant denominations affiliated with the National Council of the Churches of Christ in the U.S.A.[19] decreased as a percentage of U.S. population by 41% between 1968 and 1996. In 1968, this group included 26,446,327, or 13.2% of U.S. population. In 1996, the group included 20,489,090, or 7.7% of U.S. population.

Figure 10: **Trend in Membership as a Percent of U.S. Population, Ten Mainline Protestant Denominations, Linear and Exponential Regression Based on Data for 1968-1985, with Actual Data 1986-1996**

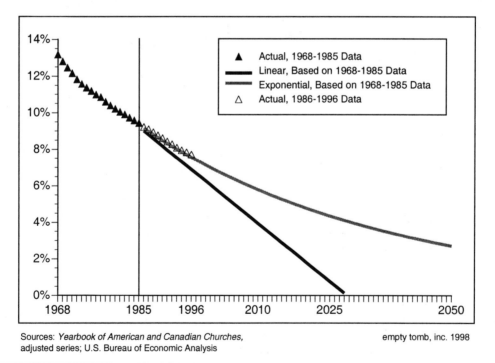

Sources: *Yearbook of American and Canadian Churches,* empty tomb, inc. 1998
adjusted series; U.S. Bureau of Economic Analysis

---

[18]The denominations analyzed in this section include the composite of 29 communions analyzed elsewhere in this report. The data for 29 communions is supplemented by the data of eight denominations included in an analysis of church membership and U.S. population by Roozen and Hadaway in David A. Roozen and Kirk C. Hadaway, eds., *Church and Denominational Growth* (Nashville: Abingdon Press, 1993), 393-395.
[19]These ten denominations include eight of the communions in the composite as well as The Episcopal Church and The United Methodist Church.

As with giving as a percentage of income to Congregational Finances and Benevolences, the 1968-1985 membership data for these ten mainline Protestant communions was analyzed using both linear and exponential regression. The actual 1986 through 1996 data was also presented. As shown in Figure 10, the actual 1986-1996 data more closely follows the exponential curve. The data would therefore suggest that these ten denominations will represent 2.7% of the U.S. population by the year 2050, a decrease of 65% from the 1996 level of 7.7%.

Membership Trends in the Composite Denominations. Eight of the ten mainline Protestant denominations discussed above are included in the composite denominations that have been considered in earlier chapters of this report. Regression analysis was carried out on the 1968-1985 data for the composite denominations to determine if the trends in the larger grouping differed from the mainline denomination subset. The results were then compared to the actual 1986 through 1996 membership data for the composite data set.

The composite denominations represented 14.1% of the U.S. population in 1968, and 12.6% in 1985. Linear trend analysis suggests that this grouping would have represented 11.74% of U.S. population in 1996, while exponential regression suggests it would have been 11.82%. In fact, this composite grouping of communions represented 11.52% of the U.S. population in 1996, a smaller figure than that indicated by linear regression, suggesting the trend is closer to that predicted by linear regression than the exponential curve.

If the trend of the last 29 years, from 1968-1996, continues uninterrupted into the future, these composite denominations would represent 7.6% of the U.S. population in the

Figure 11:   Trend in Membership as a Percent of U.S. Population, Composite Denominations, Linear and Exponential Regression Based on Data for 1968-1985, with Actual Data 1986-1996

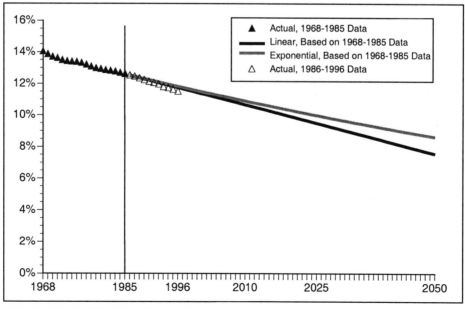

Sources: *Yearbook of American and Canadian Churches,* adjusted series; U.S. Bureau of Economic Analysis

empty tomb, inc. 1998

year 2050. This points to a decrease of 34% from 1996 levels in membership as a percent of U.S. population by the year 2050 for this set of communions. Figure 11 presents this information in graphic form.

Membership in an Expanded Set of Communions. In addition to these composite denominations, membership data for the period 1968-1996 is reviewed for seven additional Protestant communions as well, bringing the number of Protestant denominations with available data to 37. This expanded set of denominations includes some of the faster growing denominations in the U.S. When one considers whether the Protestant church in the U.S. is being marginalized as a social institution, a larger grouping of denominations provides a broader base from which to gain additional insight.

In 1968, these 37 Protestant denominations represented 42,685,587 members, and in 1996, a total of 43,616,672, an increase of 2%. Meanwhile, the overall population in the U.S. had been growing at a faster rate than the membership changes posted by these denominations. As a result, these communions were 21% of the U.S. population in 1968, and 16% in 1996.

Of course, the picture would be incomplete without the Roman Catholic Church, which included 47,468,333 members in 1968, and 61,207,914 members in 1996. Adding this membership data to that of the 37 Protestant communions considered above resulted in a total of 90,153,920 members in 1968. With the U.S. population at 200,745,000, these Christians constituted 45% of the 1968 U.S. population. By 1996, the group had grown to 104,824,586 members. However, with U.S. population having grown to 265,579,000, as of 1996, these Christians comprised 39% of the American population, a percent change of -12% from the 1968 base in the portion of the American population represented by these groups.

The Response to the Trends. As in other sectors, trend lines in church giving and membership are designed to provide an additional source of information. Planning, evaluation and creative thinking are some of the types of constructive responses which can be made in light of projections. The information on church member giving and membership trends is offered as a possible planning tool.[20] The trend lines are not considered to be dictating what must happen, but rather as providing important indicators of what might happen if present conditions continue in an uninterrupted fashion. The results of the analysis may be useful as additional input to inform decisions by church leaders in the present.

The data reflects trends that raise important implications for the future. One might liken the projection to a symptom of illness. If a person is running a temperature of 104°, the choice would be to call the doctor or hope the fever runs its course. In either case, the body is communicating that there is a condition present which requires attention. Trends in church giving and membership, if used wisely, may be of assistance in addressing conditions present in the body of Christ in the U.S.

The Potential of the Church. Trends can also be used to review historical data and calculate possibilities of what might have happened under other circumstances. For example, in chapter one, consideration is given to per member giving between 1968 and 1996. The final

---

[20]For additional discussion of the implications of the trends, see Ronsvalle and Ronsvalle, *The State of Church Giving through 1991*, pp. 61-67.

section of that chapter reviews the amount of money that would have been given if 1996 giving levels had been the same as they were in 1968.

The question may also be asked, what if giving had maintained not just the same level between 1968 and 1996 as a portion of income? Rather, what if church members had chosen to direct a greater portion of their increasing incomes to the church during this period? A classic standard for giving in the church has been a tithe, or 10% of income. Suppose congregation members chose as a goal to move toward an average of 10% giving over either a longer or shorter time frame? Two scenarios that explore this potential follow.

A Rate Equal to Income Increases for Giving to Religion. In the first scenario, an analysis could be based on the supposition that giving could have increased at the rate of change in U.S. disposable personal income between 1968 and 1996. If that had been the case, the rate of giving in 1996 as a percentage of income for the composite denominations would not have been 2.58%, but rather 5.29%. This theoretical level of giving as a percentage of income would have been 105% greater than it actually was in 1996. In this scenario, by the year 2057 giving would reach an average of 10%.

In the chapter that compares alternative giving estimates, a revised series of total giving to religion is offered. This 1968-1996 series is keyed to the 1974 Filer Commission estimate of giving to religion. The 1968-1996 annual rate of change in the composite denominations was used to calculate figures for 1968-1973 and forward for 1975-1996, thus producing estimates of total giving to religion. In the Filer-based series, the 1996 estimate for total giving to religion was $48 billion.

The present discussion considers a situation in which giving as a percentage of income in 1996 had been 5.29% as a function of church giving increasing at the same rate as income between 1968 and 1996. The ratio between the theoretical level of 5.29% and the actual level of 2.58% in giving as a percentage of income in the composite denominations is 2.047. Applying this figure to the Filer-based total giving to religion amount in 1996, the total amount of giving to religion in 1996 would have been $98 billion rather than the $48 billion it is estimated was given in the Filer-based series, an additional amount of $50 billion.

The percentage of this additional money that might have been given by the historically Christian Church—those communions such as Roman Catholic, Orthodox, mainline, evangelical, and Anabaptist, that profess a commitment to the historic tenets of the faith was calculated. It was estimated that 84% of the U.S. population identifies with the historically Christian church.[21] That percentage can be applied to the $50 billion theoretical, additional total giving to religion in 1996 noted in the scenario above. The result is that the members of these communions would have donated an additional $42 billion dollars to their churches in 1996, at this increased level of giving.

One may continue this hypothetical discussion by supposing that this additional money could have been directed not to the internal operations of the congregations, but rather

---

[21]An analysis based on information in: George H. Gallup, Jr., *Religion in America* (Princeton, NJ: The Princeton Religion Research Center, 1996), 42. This somewhat conservative estimate assumes that the religious giving was given by 100% of the U.S. population. If total religious giving comes only from the 91% of the U.S. population that claims a religious affiliation (see Gallup, p. 35), then the historically Christian component gave 92% of the total (84%/91%). In that case, $46 billion would have been given by those who identify with the historically Christian church.

to the broader mission of the church. Finally, one may suppose that denominations had adopted a proposed formula that 60% of this additional money be designated for international missions, and 20% be directed to domestic benevolences.[22] In this scenario, the 60% allocation would have meant that, in 1996, there would have been an additional $25 billion available for international outreach, and the 20% allocation would have meant an additional $8.4 billion for domestic benevolences.

Reaching the Tithe. In a second scenario, one may ask what if giving had increased from 3.12% in 1968 to 10% in 1996. This level of income being donated to the church would been 287% greater than the actual 1996 level of 2.58%. At this higher rate, instead of $48 billion, $185 billion would have been donated to religion in 1996, resulting in an additional $137 billion given to religion in the United States in 1996.

Once again, the same figure of 84% can be applied to calculate the additional activity of the historically Christian Church, had giving been at the 10% level in 1996. These church members would have given $115 billion more at an average of 10% giving in 1996. The amount available for international ministries, had 60% of this increase been directed to that category, would have been $69 billion, more than the $30-$50 billion UNICEF has estimated is needed each year to address the worst of poverty conditions and end most of the child deaths around the globe.[23] The 20% available for domestic benevolences would have amounted to $23 billion.

Figure 12 presents the two scenarios of potential church giving.

The Implications of the Hypothetical Scenarios. As the nonprofit sector receives more attention from society in general, the role it plays and can play is discussed and debated. One might review the above scenarios in order to consider the question of whether the private sector, or more specifically the church, can take on additional responsibilities toward those who are in need in the U.S.

The data suggests that, if giving had increased from the actual 1996 level to an average giving level of 10%, there could have been an additional $23 billion available assist people in need in the U.S. In theory, therefore, the church could have the resources necessary to impact domestic need, even while working at a significant level to alleviate global need in partnership with international sister churches.

If giving had increased between 1968 and 1996 at the same rate as income did, toward an eventual average level of 10%, the church would have had over $8.4 billion more in 1996 for domestic benevolences, and could have been seriously considered as a significant source of servanthood leadership for addressing poverty issues in the U.S.

---

[22]UNICEF estimates that 35,000 children under the age of five die daily around the globe, mostly from preventable poverty conditions. UNICEF also estimates that 40,000 children under the age of five die annually in the United States. These statistics indicate that the great majority of need is in countries other than the U.S. The 60%/20% formula has been used in the authors' work with congregations. For a discussion of their international and domestic strategy approaches, see John Ronsvalle and Sylvia Ronsvalle, *The Poor Have Faces* (Grand Rapids, MI: Baker Books, 1992).

[23]James P. Grant, *The State of the World's Children 1990* (New York, Oxford University Press, 1989), 67.

Figure 12: **1996 Potential Additional Church Giving, including International and Domestic Allocations: at a Rate Equal to the Change in U.S. Per Capita Disposable Personal Income, 1968-1996, and at a 1996 Average of 10% Giving**

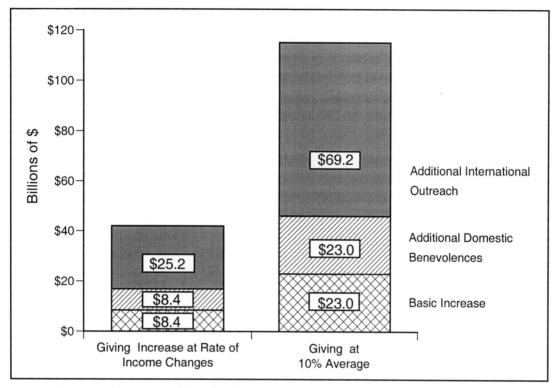

Sources: *Yearbook of American and Canadian Churches,* adjusted series; U.S. Bureau of Economic Analysis

empty tomb, inc. 1998

However, it may also be noted that giving as a percentage of income did not increase at the rate that income did between 1968 and 1996, nor had it reached the 10% level by 1996. On the contrary, giving as a percentage of income declined by 17% between 1968 and 1996. More to the point, the portion of income going to Benevolences, the category that would take into account programs that address poverty conditions in the U.S. among other issues, declined by 37% in the 1968 to 1996 period.

A discussion of the degree to which religion influences members' behavior is presented in the last chapter of this report.

Summary. The results of trend analysis do not dictate future behavior patterns, but rather indicate where present patterns are headed.

As of the 1996 data, it was not clear whether giving to Benevolences as a percentage of income paralleled a linear or exponential regression trend line. Giving to Congregational Finances followed an exponential curve more closely.

Church membership is declining as a percentage of U.S. population. The pattern is evident in a group of 10 mainline denominations, in the data set of composite denominations, and in an expanded group that includes 37 Protestant denominations and the Roman Catholic Church.

Had church giving expanded at the rate that incomes did between 1968 and 1996, or been at an average of 10% in 1996, the church would have had billions of additional dollars available to apply to domestic benevolences. In contrast to this hypothetical analysis, actual data indicates that church member giving as a percentage of income declined during the 1968 to 1996 period.

6

Denominational Reports and Other Estimates of Charitable Giving_____

The data that has been reviewed in earlier chapters results from congregation-level reports filed with the appropriate denominational office.

In addition to providing a basis for evaluating church giving trends, the data can be compared with other sources of information on philanthropy.

A major source of information is the American Association of Fund-Raising Counsel (AAFRC) Trust for Philanthropy's *Giving USA* series. This annual report provides not only an estimate of religious giving, but also an estimate of individual and total giving in the United States. Comparing the estimates developed from the denominational data series with those provided by AAFRC's series may provide additional information about the scope of the individual charitable sector in the U.S.

American Association of Fund-Raising Counsel (AAFRC) Giving USA Methodology. The annual *Giving USA* reports include an estimate for total charitable giving in the United States. The total figure includes a subtotal for individual charitable giving, which comprises somewhat over three quarters of total charitable giving. The reports also include separate estimates for charitable donations by use, such as religion, human services, and health.

AAFRC actually produces two different sets of numbers—one by sources and one by uses, or type of recipient organization—using two different methodologies, and then tries to match them. The estimate for the amount of money given by individuals is developed by an econometric model for the most recent year or two, while the use categories estimates are developed by a combination of approaches.

A difference generally occurs between the calculated total for contributions by source, which includes the amount for individual giving resulting from the econocentric model, and the total calculated receipts by different use categories. The AAFRC staff has applied different methods over the years to deal with the divergence between the projected amount given and the combined amount estimated to have been received by the use categories. For data beginning at some unstated point and continuing through 1986, any difference between the individual giving projection and the sum of the other use categories was deposited in the use category of religion, which was regarded as a "residual" category.[24] More recently, differences were attributed, at least in part, to a category labeled alternatively "Unallocated," "All Other Uses," "Undesignated" or "Unclassified."

There is also a third charitable giving estimate prepared by AAFRC, in that AAFRC routinely revises its recent historical series, as additional tax and other information is available.

AAFRC has been working to improve its estimates of giving. During 1997, AAFRC revised its methodology regarding estimates of individual giving to incorporate tax data more precisely. Therefore, as of the 1998 edition of *Giving USA*, revisions were made for the period 1985-1995. The years 1996 and 1997 were projections, because needed information for the revisions was not yet available.[25]

AAFRC also has striven to improve its use estimates. AAFRC incorporates surveys of service agencies to project a figure for many of its use categories, such as education, health and human services. In addition, in *Giving USA 1989*, AAFRC stated it revised its historical estimates for the categories of education and health. In these cases, AAFRC keyed the 1960-1972 estimates for these categories to estimates developed by the Commission on Private Philanthropy and Public Needs, commonly referred to as the Filer Commission.[26] The Filer Commission was a major national effort that resulted in a report published by the U.S. Treasury Department. A summary of the Filer report indicated that "There had been no full-scale national surveys of philanthropy prior to this study."[27] Thus, AAFRC relied on the Filer Commission estimates to provide a reference point for its historical series in the second and third largest areas of charitable activity.

Giving to Religion: Denomination-Based Series Compared to AAFRC Series. Religion is acknowledged as the single largest use category in the charitable arena. Estimates suggest about 60% of every charitable dollar donated by individuals is designated for religion.[28] If donations to other organizations that have a religious affiliation but appear in another use category—such as the Salvation Army or Catholic Social Services that are part of human services—were also considered, the portion of giving that is a function of religious activity would be higher.[29] Therefore, having an accurate estimate of giving to religion is important in determining the level of charitable financial activity in the U.S.

---

[24]Nathan Weber, *Giving USA 1990*, (New York: AAFRC Trust for Philanthropy, 1990), 187. AAFRC indicated that it revised its 1987 through 1995 data in "Methodology" 17-6 (see note 2 below for citation).

[25]Ann E. Kaplan, ed., *Giving USA 1998* (New York: AAFRC Trust for Philanthropy, 1998), 177.

[26]Nathan Weber, ed., *Giving USA 1989* (New York: AAFRC Trust for Philanthropy, 1989), 151.

[27]James N. Morgan, Richard F. Due, Judith N. Hybels, "Results from Two National Surveys of Philanthropic Activity," *History, Trends, and Current Magnitudes*, Vol. 1 in the series, *Research Papers Sponsored by The Commission on Private Philanthropy and Public Needs*, Department of the Treasury, Washington, DC, 1977, 158.

[28]AAFRC estimates that religion received 69% of individual charitable giving in 1996 ($70.66 billion of a total individual giving level of $102.35 [Kaplan, *Giving USA 1998* , 154, 156]), while Independent Sector found that 57.5% of individual giving went to religious organizations (Virginia A. Hodgkinson and Murray S. Weitzman, *Giving and Volunteering in the United States, 1996* (Washington, DC: Independent Sector, 1996), 25].

[29] For a discussion of the definition of religious charitable contributions, see Ronsvalle and Ronsvalle, "Denominational Giving Data and Other Sources of Religious Giving Information," *The State of Church Giving through 1991* (Champaign, IL: empty tomb, inc., 1993), 53-57.

The Filer Commission produced an estimate of giving to religion. That report estimated that in 1974, giving to religion was $11.7 billion.[30] This estimate was relatively close to the AAFRC estimate for 1974 of $11.84 billion.[31]

When revising its historical series, AAFRC did not choose to key its religion data to the Filer Commission estimate of giving to religion.

AAFRC did revise its religion estimates for 1987 through 1996 based on the percent change in receipts for denominations that publish data in the *Yearbook of American and Canadian Churches* series.[32]

In theory, one could follow a methodology for religion similar to that AAFRC used for the categories of education and health, in this case keying 1974 to the Filer Commission estimate, and then calculate estimates for the years 1968 to 1973, and 1975 to 1996, based on an external source of data. The external source of data could be the same that AAFRC used to revise its 1987 through 1996 data, a set of denominations that publish data in the *Yearbook of American and Canadian Churches* series. This revised approach would remedy the estimates for those years when AAFRC did not calculate a figure for religion, but rather considered it a "residual" category, having the use category of religion absorb the difference between AAFRC's estimate of total giving and the sum of its estimates for other use categories.

The starting base in this approach could be the Filer Commission estimate of $11.7 billion for 1974. The amount of change from year to year, calculated for 1968 to 1973 and also 1975 to 1996, could be the annual percentage change in the 29 denominations analyzed in other chapters of this report. This calculation yields a total of $8 billion given to religion in 1968, and $48 billion in 1996. These figures contrast with the AAFRC estimate of $8.42 billion in 1968 and $70.66 billion in 1996. Table 16 presents this data.

Comparing these two estimate series, one may observe that the two series are within a few percentage points of each other for two years on either side of 1974, the year of the Filer estimate to which the denominational-based series is keyed. The estimates vary from 11% to 13% through 1981. AAFRC methodology does not indicate when religion became a residual use category, although the differences in the data series suggests some change in AAFRC methodology took place between 1976 and 1977.

In 1982, while the denominational-based estimate series continues to change at a consistent rate, the AAFRC estimate series begins to expand more rapidly from year to year. The percentage difference grew from 17% in 1982 to 48% in 1996.

---

[30]*Research Papers Sponsored by The Commission on Private Philanthropy and Public Needs, Vol. 1, History, Trends, and Current Magnitudes*, Department of the Treasury, Washington, DC, 1977, 136.
[31]Kaplan, *Giving USA 1993*, 156.
[32]On page 179 of *Giving USA,* AAFRC suggests that its 1986 data matches that of other religion sources. The 1986 estimate is close to the estimate in the first edition of the Independent Sector report, *From Belief to Commitment* by Virginia A. Hodgkinson, Murray Weitzman, and Arthur D. Kirsch, eds. (Washington, DC: Independent Sector, 1988). However, the next Independent Sector figure in Virginia A. Hodgkinson, Murray Weitzman, et al., *From Belief to Commitment* (Washington, DC: Independent Sector, 1992) varied from the AAFRC estimate. For a discussion of the latter data, see Ronsvalle and Ronsvalle, *The State of Church Giving through 1991*, 41-42.

Table 16: **Giving to Religion, AAFRC Series and Denomination-Based Series, 1968-1996, Aggregate, Billions of Dollars and Percent Difference**

Year	AAFRC Series (Billions $)	Denomination-Based Series Keyed to 1974 Filer Series (Billions $)	Percent Difference between AAFRC and Denomination-Based Series
1968	$8.42	$8.01	5%
1969	$9.02	$8.33	8%
1970	$9.34	$8.66	8%
1971	$10.07	$9.14	10%
1972	$10.10	$9.79	3%
1973	$10.53	$10.70	-2%
1974	$11.84	$11.70	1%
1975	$12.81	$12.75	0%
1976	$14.18	$13.87	2%
1977	$16.98	$15.02	13%
1978	$18.35	$16.41	12%
1979	$20.17	$18.14	11%
1980	$22.23	$20.07	11%
1981	$25.05	$22.14	13%
1982	$28.06	$23.99	17%
1983	$31.84	$25.67	24%
1984	$35.55	$27.77	28%
1985	$38.21	$29.46	30%
1986	$41.68	$31.16	34%
1987	$43.51	$32.51	34%
1988	$45.15	$33.76	34%
1989	$47.77	$35.57	34%
1990	$49.79	$37.11	34%
1991	$50.00	$38.50	30%
1992	$54.91	$39.58	39%
1993	$56.29	$40.65	38%
1994	$60.21	$43.51	38%
1995	$66.26	$45.58	45%
1996	$70.66	$47.80	48%

Details in the above table may not compute to the numbers shown due to rounding.

Although AAFRC revised its data for 1987 through 1996 based on a different methodology than the residual definition, those latter estimates continued to build on the earlier years' data, during which religion was a residual category absorbing any difference between AAFRC's individual giving estimate and its sum of the other use category estimates.

Total Charitable Giving: Denomination-Based Series Compared to AAFRC Series. The historical series of denomination-based data keyed to the Filer Commission can be used to consider an alternative estimate of total charitable giving.

The use categories, other than religion, are generally based on surveys of large organizations within the activity definition, such as the Council for Aid to Education in the category of education, and the Association of Healthcare Philanthropy in the area of health. When such combined data is not available, according to the AAFRC methodology, AAFRC staff surveys organizations within the particular category.[33] These specific data are then extrapolated to represent the entire category.

One method for developing an alternative estimate to AAFRC's total charitable giving series would be to subtract the published AAFRC religion series from its published total contributions series. The denomination-based figures that are keyed to the Filer Commission 1974 estimate can then be added to the remaining sum of the other use categories. In this way, a revised series is developed for total charitable giving. One advantage of this revised series is that it is based on an explicit methodology for the important subcategory of religion.

The resulting figures suggest that $110.6 billion was given to charity in 1996 from all sources, as compared to the estimate of $133.5 billion in the published AAFRC series.

Individual Charitable Giving: Denomination-Based Series Compared to AAFRC Series. Individual giving makes up the major portion of giving to religion: "Most giving to religion comes from individuals. Some giving to religion also comes from bequests, and about two percent of foundation grants go to religion."[34] Therefore, while a revised series for religion affects the total charitable giving estimate, the effect would be more pronounced in the category of total individual giving, where, based on AAFRC estimates, more than sixty cents of every dollar is donated to religion.

To develop a revised estimate of individual giving, the AAFRC estimate of giving to religion can be subtracted from the AAFRC total of individual giving. This methodology is only approximate since, as AAFRC notes, some giving to religion comes from bequests—an amount not noted in the AAFRC methodology—and about 2% of foundation grants are also donated to religion. In 1996, at the 2% level, the foundation grants would have amounted to $240 million dollars.[35] Without more specific data about the source of contributions provided by AAFRC in its methodology, attributing 100% of religion to individual giving provides an initial basis for comparison.

The AAFRC giving to religion series was subtracted from the AAFRC individual giving series. The denomination-based series keyed to the Filer Commission estimate was then added to the resulting AAFRC individual series from which the AAFRC giving to religion series had been subtracted.

The revised individual denomination-based giving series suggests that individuals gave $79.49 billion to charity in 1996, compared to the published AAFRC estimate of $102 billion.

---

[33]Kaplan, *Giving USA 1998*, 179-180.

[34]Ann E. Kaplan, ed., *Giving USA 1996* (New York: American Association of Fund-Raising Counsel Trust for Philanthropy, 1996), 101. See also Kaplan, *Giving USA 1998*, 84.

[35]The 1996 AAFRC estimate for foundations was $12.00 billion. Two percent of that amount would be $240 million dollars. Total bequests in 1996 was estimated to have been $11.48 billion. See Kaplan, *Giving USA 1998*, 154.

Again, the advantage of the revised series that includes the denomination-based religion estimate is that the large component of religion that comprises somewhat over 60% of total individual gifts, is based on data reported by over 100,000 of the estimated 350,000 religious congregations of any type in the United States.

The AAFRC Econocentric Model for Individual Giving. AAFRC is to be commended for working to improve its information series, one of the key sources of general charitable giving patterns in the United States.

During 1997, AAFRC consulted with various sources to improve the econocentric model that produces its estimate of individual giving. As a result, AAFRC published a revised data series in *Giving USA 1998*.

It should also be noted that the two most recent years in *Giving USA 1998* are projections. The IRS data needed to produce 1997 estimates through the econocentric model was not available in time for the *Giving USA 1998* deadline. In *Giving USA 1998*, the model for 1996 "accounts for itemized deductions on tax returns, personal income, and the stock market value at year-end. For 1997, a year for which there are not statistics yet available from IRS, only income and the stock market data are used in the regression."[36] When income and the stock market have increased at the end of the year, the projection for charitable giving will of necessity increase.

The AAFRC econocentric model may be a useful tool for developing a working estimate of charitable giving for the most recent year. However, the public and media should be aware that, as indicated in the "Executive Statement and Overview" of *Giving USA 1998*, the numbers announced for the most recent years are forecasts based on past behavior. These numbers do not necessarily accurately reflect the direction or degree of any change in actual giving patterns.

Aggregate Compared with Per Capita Data. AAFRC data is generally considered in aggregate numbers. These totals indicate how much various charitable categories, such as Human Services or Education, had received. The focus of the present report is on trends in individual giving. For this reason, a review of the AAFRC data converted to a per capita basis may be useful.

Per capita data takes into account not only the changes in the amounts given, but also changes in the population of donors.

When the AAFRC data—the series as published rather than the revised denomination-based series discussed above—takes population into account, the positive trend noted from year to year is affected.

In current dollars, according to the AAFRC aggregate individual data, giving increased from $14.75 billion in 1968 to $102.35 billion in 1996. When those aggregate numbers are divided by the population, the figures also show an increase on a per capita basis. In 1968, according to this data, per capita giving was $73.48 and in 1996, it was $385.38.

Similarly, current dollar per member giving increased in the composite denominations, as shown in Table 1 of this report's chapter one.

---

[36]Kaplan, *Giving USA 1998*, 175.

Giving as a Percent of Income. One telling indicator in an evaluation of philanthropy is how much a contribution represents of the individual's overall income. In this way, one might attribute a weight to the value that people place on charitable activity in the context of their total spending patterns.

In 1968, U.S. per capita disposable personal income in current dollars was $3,101, and in 1996 it was $20,840. Disposable personal income is the category of choice because it takes into account the change in personal taxes during the 1968-1996 period. Although AAFRC does consider individual giving as a portion of income, it uses personal income which does not reflect changes in the level of taxes paid by individuals donating to charity.[37]

Per Capita Individual Giving as a Percent of Income. When the per capita AAFRC estimate of individual giving is taken as a portion of income, it becomes apparent that in 1968, charitable giving represented 2.37% of each American's income, while in 1996 it represented 1.85%, a decline of 22% in the portion of U.S. per capita disposable personal income contributed to charity.

If the revised series of individual giving—substituting the denomination-based series for the AAFRC estimate of giving to religion—is used, we find that per capita individual giving was $71.42 in 1968 and $299.31 in 1996. When these amounts are taken as a portion of U.S. per capita disposable personal income, the percent of per capita income donated to charity declined from 2.30% in 1968 to 1.44% in 1996, a decline of 38%.

Per Capita Giving to Religion. The aggregate data in Table 16 was divided by U.S. population to produce a per capita figure for both the AAFRC giving to religion series and the denomination-based series. The two series were then converted to giving as a percentage of U.S. disposable personal income. The comparison is presented in Figure 13 below.

Figure 13: **Per Capita Giving to Religion, AAFRC Series and Denomination-Based Series, 1968-1996, as a Percentage of U.S. Per Capita Disposable Personal Income**

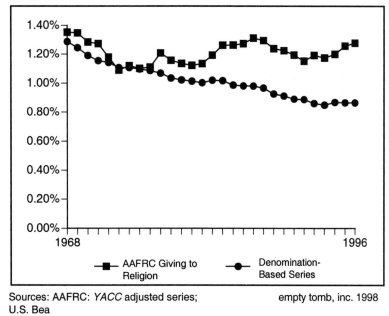

Sources: AAFRC: *YACC* adjusted series;   empty tomb, inc. 1998
U.S. Bea

[37]Kaplan, *Giving USA 1998*, 34.

Per Capita Giving to Other Use Categories, 1968-1996. Considering giving to various use categories on a per capita basis as well may provide a different picture than indicated by the aggregate data. A comparison is presented in Table 17 below.

It should be noted that the use categories presented by AAFRC do not make a distinction by source of contribution. AAFRC does state that the majority of donations to religion comes from individuals. However, AAFRC does not provide figures within each of the various use categories as to the amount of donations from each source, the four being: corporations, bequests, foundations, and individuals. Therefore, the comparison below is only approximate. It does, however, suggest important factors to be taken into consideration when discussing trends in charitable giving.

Table 17 presents the AAFRC published data for the use categories of: religion; education; health; human services; arts, culture, and humanities; and public/society benefit.[38] Since data for the use categories of environment/wildlife and international affairs is provided only for years beginning with 1987, these categories are not included. The category of giving

Table 17: **AAFRC Giving to Use Categories, 1968 and 1996, Aggregate, Current and Inflation-adjusted 1997 Dollars (Billions of Dollars), and Per Capita as a Percent of U.S. Disposable Personal Income, with Percent Change 1968-1996**

	Religion			Education		
	Aggregate (Billions $)		Per Capita	Aggregate (Billions $)		Per Capita
	Current $	Infl.-Adj.'97 $	% Income	Current $	Infl.-Adj.'97 $	% Income
1968	$8.42	$38.83	1.35%	$2.38	$10.98	0.38%
1996	$70.66	$72.28	1.28%	$19.16	$19.59	0.35%
% Change	739%	86%	-6%	705%	78%	-9%

	Health			Human Services		
	Aggregate (Billions $)		Per Capita	Aggregate (Billions $)		Per Capita
	Current $	Infl.-Adj.'97 $	% Income	Current $	Infl.-Adj.'97 $	% Income
1968	$2.08	$9.59	0.33%	$2.31	$10.65	0.37%
1996	$13.89	$14.21	0.25%	$12.16	$12.44	0.22%
% Change	568%	48%	-25%	426%	17%	-41%

	Arts, Culture, and Humanities			Public/Society Benefit		
	Aggregate (Billions $)		Per Capita	Aggregate (Billions $)		Per Capita
	Current $	Infl.-Adj.'97 $	% Income	Current $	Infl.-Adj.'97 $	% Income
1968	$0.60	$2.79	0.10%	$0.43	$1.97	0.07%
1996	$10.92	$11.17	0.20%	$7.57	$7.74	0.14%
% Change	1708%	300%	103%	1669%	293%	99%

---

[38]Kaplan, *Giving USA 1998*, 156-159. A cursory review of *Giving USA 1998* did not indicate what deflator was used to convert the current dollar figures on pp. 156-157 to inflation-adjusted dollars on pp. 158-159. The per capita figures in Table 17 were calculated by empty tomb, inc.

to foundations has current dollar data only back to 1978, and likewise is not considered in this table. The category of unallocated is also not included.

From this table, it is apparent once again that giving to religion receives the highest level of charitable giving support. Aggregate giving in both current and inflation-adjusted dollars increased. However, as a portion of U.S. per capita disposable personal income, the amount of giving to religion decreased by 6%. Table 17 uses the AAFRC estimate of giving to religion series. When the denomination-based series data was used instead, the portion of U.S. disposable personal income donated to religion declined from 1.29% in 1968 to 0.86% in 1996, a decline of 33%.

All the categories in Table 17 showed an increase in terms of aggregate giving in both current and inflation-adjusted dollars. However, giving as a percentage of income provides additional information. Per capita giving as a portion of income to education decreased 9% during this period, health decreased 25%, and giving to human services declined 41%.

Figure 14 presents two views of five use categories: education; health; human services; arts, culture, and humanities; and public/society benefit. The view in the left column presents the aggregate AAFRC data in both current and inflation-adjusted 1997 dollars. This is the view presented in the *Giving USA* series for each use category. The view in the right column for each use category presents the AAFRC data on a per capita basis as a percentage of U.S. per capita disposable personal income.

The decline to human services as a portion of per capita disposable personal income is an important indicator. Often, when the trends in religious giving discussed in other chapters of this report are presented, a frequent question from the listeners is whether individuals have withdrawn giving from their churches and directed it to other helping agencies. Since giving to religion declined by 6% using the AAFRC published series, or by 33% using the revised denomination-based series—while per capita giving to human services declined by 41% as a portion of income—the data does not support the conventional wisdom that giving to religion has decreased because there was a withdrawal from religious giving in favor of specialized human service agencies.

The two use categories that show an increase are arts, culture and humanities, and the category of public/society benefit. While neither group represented more than 0.2% of per capita giving as a portion of income in 1996, both posted increases between 1968 and 1996, in contrast to the other categories in the table.

The Need for Data Sources for the AAFRC Estimate of Giving. A detailed presentation of the data from which AAFRC prepares the *Giving USA* series would be helpful to both researchers and journalists in their attempts to inform the general public. Nine categories plus the category of "unallocated" are included in *Giving USA*. It is difficult to evaluate AAFRC's data over time without information, in tabular form, such as: the source (individual, corporate, foundation, bequest) of contributions to a given use category; the amount from that source; the numerical data which served as a basis for the source estimate within each use category, in adequate detail. AAFRC does not currently publish this data in its *Giving USA* series.

Summary. The American Association of Fund-Raising Counsel, Inc. (AAFRC) publishes the annual *Giving USA* series. AAFRC actually produces two estimates of giving

Figure 14:   AAFRC Use Category Data, 1968-1996

Giving to Education

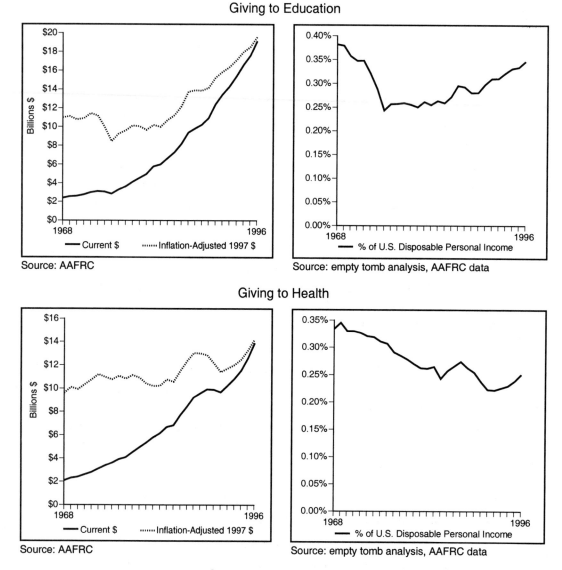

Source: AAFRC

Source: empty tomb analysis, AAFRC data

Giving to Health

Source: AAFRC

Source: empty tomb analysis, AAFRC data

Giving to Human Services

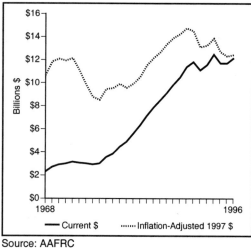

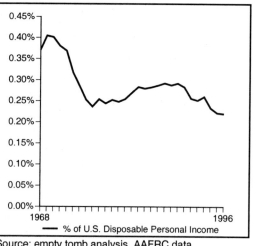

Source: AAFRC

Source: empty tomb analysis, AAFRC data

Figure 14:   AAFRC Use Category Data, 1968-1996, Continued

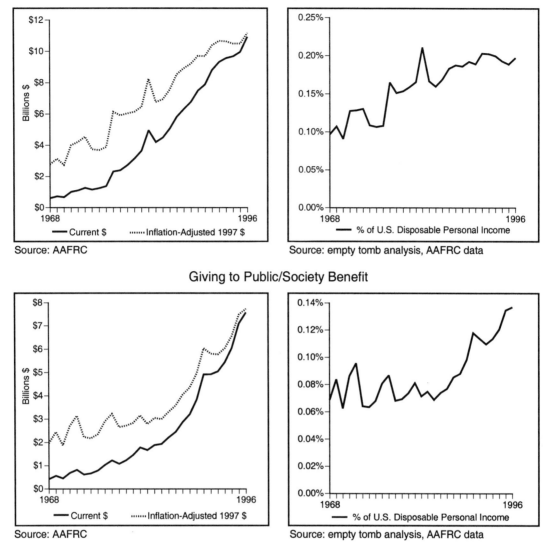

Giving to Arts, Culture, and Humanities

Source: AAFRC

Source: empty tomb analysis, AAFRC data

Giving to Public/Society Benefit

Source: AAFRC

Source: empty tomb analysis, AAFRC data

for the most recent year. One is a projection based on an econocentric model to produce an estimate for individual contributions. This individual giving projection is combined with estimates for bequests, foundations, and corporations to produce a total charitable giving estimate by source of contribution. A second estimate of giving for the most recent year is defined by use of contribution, including surveys within some use categories. Any discrepancy between the two totals has, in the past, been assigned to either religion or another use category, such as "undesignated" or "unclassified."

Since AAFRC revises its past data, notably individual giving, as additional information becomes available, this revised series comprises a third estimate within the *Giving USA* series.

When a 1968-1996 denomination-based series keyed to the Filer Commission 1974 estimate of giving to religion was compared to the AAFRC series, the 1996 AAFRC estimate for giving to religion of $70.7 billion was 48% higher than the denomination-based series estimate of $47.8 billion. As would be expected, a similar $23 billion difference was reflected when the same denomination-based series was used to revise the AAFRC total charitable giving estimate series and the individual giving series.

The AAFRC data was also considered on a per capita basis, to account for population changes, and as a portion of U.S. per capita disposable personal income, to account for the changes in taxes during the 1968-1996 period. Per capita giving to the four largest AAFRC use categories indicated a decline as a portion of income between 1968 and 1996.

7

Church Member Giving in Perspective: Can Religion Influence the Middle Class?_____

Religion's ability to impact poverty has been rediscovered.

• A June 1, 1998 *Newsweek* cover asked, "What's the Hottest Idea In Crime Fighting?" Answering its own question was the announcement, "The Power of Religion."

• Columnist George Will pointed to Deliverance Evangelistic Church in Philadelphia as one example of "faith-based approaches to social problems."[39]

• An article in *The Christian Century* reviewed the economic strategies growing out of the Christian Economic Coalition of Boston, focusing on entrepreneurial activity in the poorest areas of the city.[40]

• The Institute for Black Family Development, based in Detroit, Michigan, was formed to work with pastors and other religious workers "to meet the spiritual needs of African-American families," according to an article in *Christianity Today*. One leader interviewed for the story noted that the present generation is the first to live without the formal legal constraints of segregation. Pastors previously protected parishioners from the devastating effects of slavery and then segregation, according to Rev. DeForest Soaries, and it has taken time for them to recognize the role they have to play as the circumstances have changed.[41]

• In an article in *World* magazine, Don Taylor, head of Mississippi's Department of Human Services, recognizes his state agency was ahead of the curve in developing the "Faith and Families" program that matches welfare clients with supportive congregations. The 1996 welfare reform package included the Ashcroft amendment, also known as Charitable Choice, allowing faith-based groups, including churches, to receive federal funds to support their anti-poverty work. " 'By the time Charitable Choice came along, we were already doing this,' he says."[42]

---

[39]George Will, "Urban Churches Have Solution," *Champaign (Ill.) News-Gazette*, September 6, 1996, A-4.
[40]S. Mark Heim, "God's Long Shot in the Inner City: A Vision of Church-Based Economic Development," *The Christian Century*, July 5-12, 1995, 680-681.
[41]Kim Lawton with Tammy Blackard, "Giving Black Families a Boost," *Christianity Today*, 38-39.
[42]Roy Maynard and Bob Jones IV, "Fighting Poverty in Jesus' Name . . . and With Taxpayer Funds?" *World*, August 15, 1998, 12-15.

A recent conference on "Can Churches Save the Inner City?" has raised the issue of religion impacting poverty-based behaviors to respectable levels. According to a report about the conference, in 1986 a study pointed to a relationship between religion and the decrease in delinquency of poor inner city youth, but was largely ignored at that time. The issue is still controversial among academics, but there is a growing acknowledgment that the impact of religion on behaviors and conditions that reinforce poverty is worth review.[43]

John Wesley noticed the correlation when he observed, "For religion must necessarily produce both industry and frugality."[44] Indeed, Wesley's work, as well as that of others such as William Booth who founded the Salvation Army, focused on those most forgotten by the societies in which they lived, and the transforming power of religion in their lives.

The current attention on the role of faith-based organizations in addressing some of the thorniest social problems in American society is a return to a long-recognized approach. Religion continues to have a role to play in the lives of the poor minority inhabiting this affluent society, giving those in need hope and focus when so many other factors seem arrayed against them.

A different question may confront contemporary American society. For the sake of argument, the ability of religion to transform the lives of the poor may be granted. The larger question for a country where the poor have become a relatively small percentage of the population is, can religion influence the vast middle class?

In fact, John Wesley's comment cited above did not focus on the poor. Rather, his bigger concern was what he termed the "continual declension of pure religion." He noted that the good behaviors that accompany the religious experience result in positive fruits. He went on to write that industry and frugality "cannot but produce riches. But as riches increase, so will pride, anger, and love of the world in all its branches." He was concerned about what to do so that "our money may not sink us to the nethermost hell."[45]

Spending priorities. Wesley's concern about the role of money in the lives of the faithful echoed the warnings from the founder of the faith, Jesus Christ. In the Sermon on the Mount, Jesus presented a choice to those who would follow him. People can serve God or money, he said, narrowing the options to only two in Matthew 6:24. Just three verses before, Jesus observed that "where your treasure is, there your heart will be also" (Matt. 6:21, NIV).

The data in the previous chapters of this report indicates church members have been tempered in the amount of increase they have directed to their churches from one year to the next. A review of consumer spending patterns suggest that this giving pattern is not due to a lack of resources available to church members.

It may be noted that there is an awkwardness present when considering church member giving in light of consumer spending patterns in the U.S. The difficulty, of course, is that currently there is no data indicating whether those making particular purchases are church members or not. General spending data includes both those affiliated with churches, and those who are not. Two points may mitigate this concern.

---

[43]David Boldt, a Knight Ridder article appearing as "Keeping the Faith" in *Champaign (Ill.) News-Gazette*, November 22, 1998, B-1 and B-5.

[44]Herbert Welch, ed., *Selections from the Writings of John Wesley* (Nashville: Abingdon, 1942), 208.

[45]Welch, 208.

First, the types of consumer expenditures reviewed can be limited to those that are as likely as not to be made by church members. A decision has been made in the present discussion not to include what might be called "sin expenditures" that at least some church members might avoid on religious grounds. Thus, the $31 billion spent on cigars, cigarettes and other tobacco, or the $58 billion spent on alcoholic beverages[46] will not be considered.[47]

The issue of gambling would also seem removed from the present discussion, with the possible exception of state lotteries that have led some to believe that participation in this activity is actually a way to further funding of education. It may be noted in passing that in 1996, $586.5 billion was wagered, with $47.6 billion the net revenue for the industry.[48]

The second mitigating factor in a general discussion of consumer expenditures is the large percentage of church membership in the United States. According to the Princeton Research Center, 84% of the U.S. population cites a historically Christian tradition as its religious preference. Membership in these groups would be upwards of 60% of the entire population.[49] Thus, church members are broadly involved in the American economy, including consumer purchases.

While a variety of consumer expenditures could be mentioned to develop a sense of scale in terms of church member giving, the present discussion will touch on only three: pets; eating habits; and selected outdoor recreation activities.

Pets. Pets are common since almost 60% of the households in the U.S. have at least one.[50] The American Pet Products Manufacturers Association, Inc. estimated that $21.3 billion was spent on pets in 1996,[51] close to one-quarter to one-half of total religious giving estimates.

However, society being as busy as it is leaves less time for human family members, to say nothing of pets. Concerned owners can invest in pet sitting services so their animal friends will not feel forsaken in their absence. One industrious pet sitter noted that when she started in 1983, she may have been one of the first in the field, but as of 1997 there were 1600 participants in the association she started.[52]

Perhaps it is guilt about not having enough quality time that spawned the Sierra Mountain Doggie Camp where the canine friend can swim, hike, and be met at the airport for $1,500 per week. The definition of "treats" has also changed with the advent of $21 per pound gourmet snack foods.[53] Accessories are available not only for dogs and cats but ferrets, who

---

[46]U.S. Bureau of the Census, *Statistical Abstract of the United States: 1997* (117th ed.) (Washington, DC: 1997), 768.

[47]A pastor called after one presentation to inquire for these "sin expenditures" because, he noted, about half his congregation was "wet."

[48]"Growth in Gaming Industry Slowed Last Year in Both Handle and Revenue," *International Gaming & Wagering Business Magazine* via www.igwb.com/news/gaw.html.

[49]George H. Gallup, Jr., *Religion in America 1996* (Princeton, NJ: The Princeton Religion Research Center), 41-42. The estimate of 60% of the population affiliated with historically Christian churches is an adjustment of the total of 69% of members in all religious traditions in the U.S.

[50]Pet Ecology Brands, Inc. Homepage at www.petecology.com/products.htm.

[51]Pamela Hobbs, "From Wild to Mild" at www.abcnews.com/sections/us/pets/pets_intro.html.

[52]Susan Herrell, "Some Pets Sitting Pretty," *Champaign (Ill.) News-Gazette*, April 21, 1997, B-1, B-6.

[53]Carol Lloyd, "How Much Is That Doggie . . . " *MoJowire* of MotherJones, March/April 1998 at www.mojones.com/mother_jones/MA98/doggie.html.

might look particularly spiffy in a black leather biker jacket, or hamsters who perhaps would enjoy the delicacy of a Hamster Potty.[54]

Because there is a concern to provide good health care for pets, a few companies are now offering pet insurance. Veterinary medicine has advanced, and the concerned owner can obtain a kidney transplant or hip replacement for a loved pet.[55] As with human illness, medical insurance for pets is designed to take some of the sting out of an already painful situation. One company did not believe it when they first heard about this type of policy, but now finds the insurance one of its bigger sellers.[56]

Eating Habits. "Eating places" posted $224 billion in sales in 1996.[57] That works out to $842 a year for every person in the U.S., compared to average church member giving of $538.

A segment of the food industry that is growing rapidly is what is termed "home-meal replacement." These foods range from frozen dinners to services that cater a set number of meals per week for busy people who want to eat home-cooked food at home but are too busy to prepare it themselves. These services are estimated to grow to $67 billion in 1998.[58]

Health has become an increasing concern for the American consumer. Americans may like snack foods enough to pay $15 billion a year for them, but consumers don't want the foods to contribute to unwanted pounds. Thus, the fastest growing facet of the industry is " 'healthy' junk food."[59]

Another rapidly growing category is food supplements. Minerals, herbal supplements, sports nutrition, vitamins, and diet ads were projected to grow to $6 billion in 1996, up from about $750 million in 1991.[60]

Outdoor Recreation. Leisure activities fill the empty places in Americans' nonworking time. Gardening had blossomed into a $25 billion dollar industry in 1996.[61] Hunters increased their expenditures by 78 percent between 1991 and 1996, up to $22.1 billion.[62] Personal watercraft sales grew from 48,000 in 1988 to 191,000 in 1996, an increase of 300%.[63]

For the truly adventurous, who want to go not just outdoors but out of this world, there will soon be the option to take a 15-minute ride into outer space, including experiencing weightlessness, for $3,500 a trip.[64]

---

[54]"An Accessory Too Far," a June 9, 1997 Associated Press story at wp4.washingtonpost.com/wp-srv/digest/daily/june/21/pets.htm.

[55]"Health Care for You and Your Pet: A Comparison" at msnbc.com/onair/nbc/nightlynews/PetSurgery/default.asp.

[56]An Associated Press story appearing as "Pet Insurance Booming Business," *Champaign (Ill.) News-Gazette*, November 4, 1998, B-6.

[57]*U.S. Statistical Abstract: 1997*, 769.

[58]An Associated Press story appearing as "Illinois Firm Sees Big Sales in Fresh, Ready-to-Eat Meals," *Champaign (Ill.) News-Gazette*, November 24, 1998, B-2.

[59]Laura Shapiro, "Fake Fat: Miracle or Menace?" *Newsweek*, January 8, 1996, 60.

[60]Geoffrey Cowley, "Herbal Warning," *Newsweek*, May 6, 1996, 67.

[61]"New Book Taps Into A Growing Field, Home Gardening," *USA Weekend*, March 28-30, 1997, 10.

[62]Brian Dietz, "Spending Bucks Makes Outdoors Sense," *Champaign (Ill.) News-Gazette*, May 29, 1998, C-7.

[63]"Be Safe on The Water This Summer," *USA Weekend*, June 12-14, 1998, 12.

[64]A Boston Globe article appearing as "Coming Up Soon in Tourism: Space Flights," *Champaign (Ill.) News-Gazette*, April 19, 1998, F-2.

The Influence of Religion on Church Members. These particular expenditures are probably not against the religious tenets of most faith traditions in the U.S. So it is of interest that many of these consumer purchases have shown sizable increases in recent years. Meanwhile church giving has increased only moderately, thereby not keeping up with the growth in personal incomes. The result is a shrinking market share for the church in terms of member spending patterns.

If members in general are not finding money to maintain or even increase the portion of income given to the church, while consumer expenditures are expanding, this situation may point to a lack of integration between the stated faith and the practice of spending. This divided mind-set suggests that religion has a limited practical impact on members' lives.

Other social conditions suggest a similar conclusion. The results of the 1998 election came as a surprise to many people. In April of that year, articles were appearing with headlines like "Reclaiming America, Evangelicals Vow to Take Back America, One Precinct at a Time."[65] Just after the election, an Associated Press article appeared under the headline, "Religious Right Takes Beating with '98 Election."[66]

Observers struggled to make sense of the results. George Will reviewed the election defeat of the incumbent governors of South Carolina and Alabama, both of whom opposed lotteries as a source of state revenues. Will concluded, "In these two bastions of the religious right, the public said that if virtue costs money, it costs too much."[67]

Meanwhile, *Washington Post* columnist David Broder talked to a Democratic senator and a Republican senator soon after the results were final. Independently, both offered the same analysis: given the positive economic conditions, people "didn't want to rock the boat."[68]

The issues that many thought would define the election did not, finally, carry as much weight as the desire for continued economic growth.

American Values. The high value placed on financial security among young people can be seen in the results of a survey done by the Joseph and Edna Josephson Institute of Ethics. Following up their 1996 survey with a second one in 1998, the Institute, which organizes the national "Character Counts!" movement, surveyed 20,000 middle school and high school students. Among the high school students, 63.2% indicated "My religion" is "Essential" or "Very Important," while 60.1% valued "Living up to my religious standards" similarly. Meanwhile, 60.7% of the responding students indicated "Being well off financially" was also "Essential" or "Very Important."

The survey asked the students to respond to the statement, "I am satisfied with my own ethics and character." Of those responding, 90.8% indicated they strongly agreed or agreed with the statement. Yet, respondents indicated they had evidenced negative behaviors at least once in the previous year at the following rates: 92.1% had "Lied to a parent"; 81.8% had "Lied to a teacher"; and 70.2% had "Cheated during a test in school." Michael Josephson,

---

[65]David Briggs for the Associated Press, "Reclaiming America, Evangelicals Vow to Take Back America, One Precinct at a Time," *Champaign (Ill.) News-Gazette*, April 12, 1998, B-1.

[66]An Associated Press article appearing as "Religious Right Takes Beating with '98 Election," *Champaign (Ill.) News-Gazette*, November 7, 1998, D-1.

[67]George Will, "GOP Loses Its Voice and Election," *Champaign (Ill.) News-Gazette*, Nov. 6, 1998, A-4.

[68]David Broder, "Voters' Message: Don't Rock Boat," *Champaign (Ill.) News-Gazette*, Nov. 8, 1998, B-2.

president of the "Character Counts!" Coalition, summarized the findings by declaring, "In terms of honesty and integrity, things are going from very bad to worse."[69]

Meanwhile, these teenagers and others like them are making economic decisions from within their ethical framework. It is estimated that teenagers in the U.S. have $103 billion to spend a year, and may influence as much as $139 billion in additional purchases in their families.[70]

Another study considered the basic goals of adults, and found the survey participants in tension about what they perceive to be important. The Merck Family Fund commissioned an exploration of the "Views of Americans on Consumption, Materialism, and the Environment." The July 1995 report found that 92% of the participants indicated that "Responsibility" was an "Important Guiding Principle" for themselves, but they felt only 28% of "most people in our society" felt the same. "Family Life" was valued by 91%, although they felt only 45% of the population at large would agree. "Religious Faith" was important to 66%, although they felt that only 18% of the population would regard it to be so.

A higher level of agreement between the individual survey participant and "Most People" was found on other "Important Guiding Principles." Regarding "Financial Security," 76% thought it was important and would be for 69% of the rest of the population; 64% thought "Career Success" important, and assumed 58% of the rest of the population would also; and 92% valued "Freedom" while 74% of "Most People" probably would as well.[71]

These last results produced a level of tension among the participants. The report summarized the findings as "People describe a society at odds with itself and its own most important values. They see their fellow Americans growing increasingly atomized, selfish and irresponsible; they worry that our society is losing its moral center."[72] Of those participating, 91% agreed that "The 'buy now, pay later' attitude causes many of us to consume more than we need" while 89% agreed, "Buying and consuming is the American way." Although people had great misgivings about the amount of consumption going on, many felt others should be free to spend their money as they chose. This internal conflict aggravated a deep-felt concern about the level of materialism present in society. One man is quoted as describing materialism as "the lust for wealth and power that . . . we're taught to worship." Further, the report found that "Many assert that excessive materialism is at the root of many of our social problems, such as crime and drugs."[73]

The anxiety these people felt about financial pressures is well based. According to one personal finance author, "Household credit-card debt has more than doubled in the last six years. In fact, personal bankruptcies reached a record high of 1.35 million in 1997, about eight times the rate in the Depression."[74]

---

[69]Joseph and Edna Josephson Institute of Ethics, "1998 Report Card on the Ethics of American Youth," (Marina del Rey, CA, 1998), 1, 31, 34-36, 38-39, 41.

[70]MarketSource Corporation, "Teen Marketing-Buying Habits" at www.marketsource.com/teen/research/buying.html.

[71]The Harwood Group, *Yearning for Balance: Views of Americans on Consumption, Materialism, and the Environment*, (Milton, MA: Merck Family Fund, July 1995), 3-4.

[72]The Harwood Group, *Yearning for Balance*, 1.

[73]The Harwood Group, *Yearning for Balance*, 4-6.

[74]Andrew Tobias, "Take Control of Your Credit Cards," *Parade Magazine*, November 1, 1998, 4.

Religion and Values. The divided attitudes revealed in the adults and youth in the two surveys cited above suggest that there is a lack of integration between religious profession and practice. Religion was not a vital factor for one-third of the high school students. In addition, the large percentage of those respondents who lied and cheated at least once meant that many of those who valued religion also exhibited those negative behaviors.

In the second study, almost two-thirds of the adult participants found religious faith important. Yet, somehow that influence did not help them sort out the pressures of materialism in their lives.

News reports announce a "resurgence of faith" occurring in the United States. For example, television commentator Bill Moyers wrote an article that declared "Religion is breaking out everywhere."[75]

However, there are those who view this development with reservation. Various church leaders interviewed for a *Dallas Morning News* article wondered what people mean when they say they are "religious." The president of International Awakening Ministries commented on the number of those who describe themselves as "born-again Christians." He offered, "The evidence is overwhelming that a terribly high percentage of that number could not possibly be Christians, because their lives are totally out of alignment with Christian truth."[76]

Jesuit priest Avery Dulles reviewed Catholic approaches to American culture for a Fordham University lecture given in late 1989. He noted that "consumerism" had become dominant in U.S. society, and, since Vatican II, Catholics had generally taken an approach of "accomodationism" which did not provide a clear choice for church members.[77]

Author Philip Yancey took a critical look at the concept of what has been termed "God's preferential option for the poor." He concluded that such a preference on God's part would not be due to the righteousness of the poor. Rather, many times poor people, through no choice of their own, are desperate enough to recognize God's love as good news, while those who are succeeding financially may be preoccupied with other matters. He notes that "Dependence, humility, simplicity, cooperation, and a sense of abandon are qualities greatly prized in the spiritual life, but extremely elusive for people who live in comfort." Those who are successful may rely on their own abilities, while those who are desperate because of poverty will often turn to God.[78]

A Southern Baptist leader suggests the comfort of the middle class has larger implications for American society. His concern in the recent presidential intern scandal was with the large number of people who were not particularly upset. "My concern is with the people whose response to a lack of character in our leaders is a roaring, "SO WHAT? LET THE GOOD TIMES ROLL!" As long as there are people in this country who believe that a leader's personal character makes no difference in any way, then I tell you that we are in the throes of crisis!"[79]

---

[75]Bill Moyers, "The Resurgence of Faith," *USA Weekend*, Oct. 11-13, 1996, 4.

[76]Ed Housewright for *Dallas Morning News*, "Leaders Wonder How True Believers Are," *Champaign (Ill.) News-Gazette*, April 20, 1995, C-4.

[77]Tracy Early for Catholic News Service, "Catholic and American: Accommodation to Culture Endangers Church, Says Theologian," *Peoria (Ill.) Catholic Post*, December 17, 1989, 10.

[78]Philip Yancey, "Is the Gospel Bad News for You?" an excerpt from *The Jesus I Never Knew* in *Christianity Today*, November 13, 1995, 52.

[79]Adrian Rogers, "Does Character Count? A Biblical Treatment," *SBC Life*, Journal of the Southern Baptist Convention, November 1998, 1 (Rogers' emphasis).

The inability to discern and to integrate moral values in the public square has been noted in other quarters as well. *The Christian Century* ran excerpts from the introduction to the ten-year anniversary edition of *Habits of the Heart*. The authors, Robert N. Bellah, Richard Madsen, William M. Sullivan, Ann Swidler and Steven M. Tipton, reflected on the "radical individualism" that they identified in their 1986 book. Ten years later, they discussed the role of "civic membership," a concept "that points to that critical intersection of personal identity with social identity." Having earlier identified the trend toward individualism, the authors write a decade later about the consequences this trend has had on society as a whole.[80]

David Mathews, the Kettering Foundation president, writing in *The Chronicle of Philanthropy*, introduces the concept of "civic philanthropy." Citing "unbridled cynicism" among the population, he equates this condition as the equivalent breakdown of physical infrastructures such as water and power systems. He notes that "community development requires a corresponding civil infrastructure for institutions to work, programs to function, and problems to be solved. Foundations depend on strong civil societies for their objectives to be met. If societies are weak, grant makers must invest in civil infrastructure."[81]

There may be a basis for arguing that church member giving trends could have served as an early-warning system for these developments in society. Sensitive to pressures placed on the individuals, spending patterns might well have reflected a change from community identity to individual gratification, before the collective social impact was felt. Giving as a percentage of income began to decline in the eleven denominations in 1961, three years before membership began to decline. In the same way, a downturn in the portion of income that members choose to invest in their churches could signal a movement away from religion as a defining element in life.

How to Proceed? Two communions have independently developed a similar strategy to increase communication with their adherents about basic values of the faith. Both groups have decided to organize themselves at the national level to go directly to the members in the pews.

The Presbyterian Church passed a resolution at its 1998 General Assembly that called on specific action from each member of the denomination. The particular issue was the removal of guns from private homes in light of shootings at schools. Apart from the specific issue involved in the Presbyterian resolution, the importance for the present discussion lies in the fact that the General Assembly decided to ask for action on the part of all Presbyterians, a change from the past. One leader was quoted as saying, "Its new ground is in speaking directly to Presbyterians to do something."[82]

Meanwhile, the Roman Catholic bishops in the U.S. recently developed an initiative for the Jubilee 2000 effort. The focus of the campaign is to promote charity, justice, and peace. However, rather than leaving the ideas at the national level, the bishops are organizing a visitation campaign in the parishes, in which members will be presented with a pledge card

---

[80]Robert N. Bellah, et al., "Individualism and the Crisis of Civic Membership," *The Christian Century*, May 8, 1996, 510.

[81]David Mathews, "Creating a Movement Toward 'Civil Philanthropy,' " *Chronicle of Philanthropy*, April 20, 1995, 42-43.

[82]Gustav Niebuhr, "Presbyterians Urged to Keep Handguns Out of the Home," *New York Times*, June 20, 1998, A-1.

asking them to make a commitment as a Catholic to pursue these ends in their families and other areas of their lives. Rather than general commitments, Catholics will be asked to take eight specific steps, including "pray regularly for justice and peace" as well as "give more generously to those in need at home and abroad."[83]

Both of these denominational efforts reflect a new focus on asking people in the pews to act in concrete ways. It may be that leaders cannot assume their members have shared values or understanding regarding the issues facing the church that will naturally lead to expected behaviors. Communication, and perhaps even education about basic concepts of the faith, may be required. The national leadership seems to have recognized that it needs to assist local ministers and priests in organizing efforts against the individualistic and self-oriented cultural forces that are impacting church members.

Many people acknowledge that the civic religion so dominant in American culture through the 1950s no longer exists. However, America continues to be a religious nation, as evidenced by the self-identification of many Americans with specific religious traditions. Leaders may have been coasting on an "after-glow" effect, as those traditions were handed down from one generation to another, but not experienced firsthand.

The after-glow is still visible. For example, a correlation appears to exist between regular church attendance, and volunteering and donating to charity.[84]

Other data would also support a sense of religion's influence. Two publications that track the nonprofit world, *The Chronicle of Philanthropy* and *The NonProfit Times*, annually compile lists of the largest nonprofit groups. These lists routinely exclude churches, in part because religious denominations are not required to file the government form used to compare organization incomes. Of those groups that are included in the list, two religious-based charities appear in each of the publications' top ten list. In addition, three of the top ten Human Services groups in *The Chronicle of Philanthropy*'s list are directly connected to religious communions, while a fourth is faith-based. Seven of the ten largest international groups also are religiously rooted.[85]

Even the analyses in the present report could suggest that national leaders need not be concerned. There may be signs that these patterns are turning around. Tables 1 and 2 in chapter one indicate that per member giving to Congregational Finances has taken an upturn in recent years. In addition, there may even be a slowing in the decline of giving to Benevolences as a percentage of income.

Yet, these recent improvements in church member giving could merely be a respite in the continued downward trend that has been evident during the past three decades. Only additional data from future years will determine whether church members are actually changing their giving patterns. Furthermore, there has been no evidence to suggest that church members are open to fulfilling their potential for donating billions of more dollars by increasing giving levels toward the classic standard of the tithe in order to address the desperate needs of others.

---

[83]Jerry Filteau for Catholic News Service, "Bishops Will Seek Personal Pledges," *Peoria (Ill.) Catholic Post*, November 22, 1998, 1.

[84]Virginia A. Hodgkinson and Murray S. Weitzman, *Giving and Volunteering in the United States, 1996 Edition* (Washington, DC: Independent Sector, 1996), 90-91.

[85]"A Banner Year for Big Charities," *Chronicle of Philanthropy*, November 5, 1998, 1, 31, and 42; and "The NPT 100, America's Biggest NonProfits," *NonProfit Times*, November 1998, 31 and 36.

The attitudes voiced by teenagers and adults in the two values surveys cited above, in combination with the current report's overall giving data, suggest that major infrastructure work still needs to be done among church members. These people appear to be struggling to find practical help in coping with the material pressures they face in everyday life. Church members may be experiencing a crisis of vision, rather than making a conscious decision to withdraw support from the goals of the church. Help can come in the form of communication and creative presentation of the basic concepts of the faith, designed to assist all church members in moving from seeing religion only as the performance of liturgical life passages observed in baptism, weddings, and funerals, to a dynamic faith that has the same power for change evident in the lives of those living at the margins of society.

The poor, still striving to achieve a sound standard of living, may well be more sensitive to the transforming power of religion. It is the middle class, those who have reaped the fruits of hard work and moral behavior in the form of a stable and comfortable environment, who will need to be reminded that authentic religion does not maintain but actually changes those who are open to it.

A place to begin may be in helping church members to integrate their faith and money. In this affluent culture, there are few more powerful forces than the money which people earn and spend. In Matthew 6:24, Jesus Christ seemed to indicate that making a clear choice about money would help people also clear their minds about other aspects of their relationship to God.

John Wesley struggled with the same difficulties in the church of his time, and developed a strategy that may have relevance for today.

> We ought not to forbid people to be diligent and frugal; we must exhort
> all Christians to gain all they can, and to save all they can; that is, in effect,
> to grow rich! What way then (I ask again), can we take, that our money
> may not sink us to the nethermost hell? There is one way, and there is no
> other under heaven. If those who 'gain all they can,' and 'save all they
> can,' will likewise 'give all they can,' then, the more they gain, the more
> they will grown in grace, and the more treasure they will lay up in
> heaven.[86]

---

[86] Welch, 208.

Appendixes

Appendix A: List of Denominations

Church Member Giving, 1968-1996

American Baptist Churches in the U.S.A.
Associate Reformed Presbyterian Church
   (General Synod)
Brethren in Christ Church
Christian Church (Disciples of Christ)
Church of God (Anderson, Ind.)
Church of God General Conference (Oregon, IL and
   Morrow, GA.)
Church of the Brethren (through 1995)
Church of the Nazarene
Conservative Congregational Christian Conference
Cumberland Presbyterian Church
Evangelical Congregational Church
Evangelical Covenant Church
Evangelical Lutheran Church in America
   The American Lutheran Church (merged 1987)
   Lutheran Church in America (merged 1987)
Evangelical Lutheran Synod
Evangelical Mennonite Church
Fellowship of Evangelical Bible Churches
Free Methodist Church of North America
Friends United Meeting (through 1990)
General Association of General Baptists
Lutheran Church-Missouri Synod
Mennonite Church
Moravian Church in America, Northern Province
North American Baptist Conference
The Orthodox Presbyterian Church
Presbyterian Church (U.S.A.)
Reformed Church in America
Seventh-day Adventists
Southern Baptist Convention
United Church of Christ
Wisconsin Evangelical Lutheran Synod

Church Member Giving, 1995–1996

The Denominations included in the 1968-1996
   analysis with data available for both years plus the
   following:
Albanian Orthodox Diocese of America
Allegheny Wesleyan Methodist Connection
   (Original Allegheny Conference)
Baptist Missionary Association of America
Church of Lutheran Brethren of America
Church of the Lutheran Confession
Churches of God General Conference

The Episcopal Church
The Evangelical Presbyterian Church
International Pentecostal Church of Christ
The Latvian Evangelical Lutheran Church in America
The Missionary Church
National Association of Free Will Baptists
Primitive Methodist Church in the U.S.A.
United Brethren in Christ
The United Methodist Church
The Wesleyan Church

By Organizational Affiliation: NAE, 1968-1996

Brethren in Christ Church
Church of the Nazarene
Conservative Congregational Christian Conference
Evangelical Congregational Church
Evangelical Mennonite Church
Fellowship of Evangelical Bible Churches
Free Methodist Church of North America
General Association of General Baptists

By Organizational Affiliation: NCC, 1968-1996

American Baptist Churches in the U.S.A.
Christian Church (Disciples of Christ)
Evangelical Lutheran Church in America
Moravian Church in America, Northern Province
Presbyterian Church (U.S.A.)
Reformed Church in America
United Church of Christ

Eleven Denominations, 1921-1996

American Baptist (Northern)
Christian Church (Disciples of Christ)
Church of the Brethren
The Episcopal Church
Evangelical Lutheran Church in America
   The American Lutheran Church
     American Lutheran Church
     The Evangelical Lutheran Church
     United Evangelical Lutheran Church
     Lutheran Free Church
   Evangelical Lutheran Churches, Assn. of
   Lutheran Church in America
     United Lutheran Church
       General Council Evangelical Lutheran Ch.

General Synod of Evangelical Lutheran Ch.
United Synod Evangelical Lutheran South
American Evangelical Lutheran Church
Augustana Lutheran Church
Finnish Lutheran Church (Suomi Synod)
Moravian Church in America, Northern Province
Presbyterian Church (U.S.A.)
United Presbyterian Church in the U.S.A.
Presbyterian Church in the U.S.A.
United Presbyterian Church in North America
Presbyterian Church in the U.S.
Reformed Church in America
Southern Baptist Convention
United Church of Christ
Congregational Christian
Congregational
Evangelical and Reformed
Evangelical Synod of North America/German
Reformed Church in the U.S.
The United Methodist Church
The Evangelical United Brethren
The Methodist Church
Methodist Episcopal Church
Methodist Episcopal Church South
Methodist Protestant Church

Conservative Cong. Christian Conf.
Cumberland Presbyterian Church
Evangelical Congregational Church
Evangelical Covenant Church
Evangelical Lutheran Synod
Evangelical Mennonite Church
Fellowship of Evan. Bible Churches
Free Methodist Church of North America
Friends United Meeting
General Association of General Baptists
Lutheran Church-Missouri Synod
Mennonite Church
North American Baptist Conference
The Orthodox Presbyterian Church
Salvation Army
Seventh-day Adventists
Southern Baptist Convention
Wisconsin Evangelical Lutheran Synod

Trends in Membership, 10 Mainline Protestant Denominations, 1968-1996

American Baptist Churches in the U.S.A.
Christian Church (Disciples of Christ)
Church of the Brethren
The Episcopal Church
Evangelical Lutheran Church in Am.
Moravian Church in America, Northern Prov.
Presbyterian Church (U.S.A.)
Reformed Church in America
United Church of Christ
The United Methodist Church

Trends in Membership, Add 27 Denominations, 1968-1996

Assemblies of God
Associate Reformed Presby. Ch (Gen Synod)
Baptist General Conference
Brethren in Christ Church
Christian and Missionary Alliance
Church of God (Anderson, IN)
Church of God (Cleveland, Tenn.)
Church of God, Gen. Conf. (Oregon, IL
and Morrow, GA)
Church of the Nazarene

Appendix B Series: Denominational Data Tables

Introduction

The data in the following tables is from the *Yearbook of American and Canadian Churches* (*YACC*) series unless otherwise noted. Financial data is presented in current dollars.

The Appendix B tables are described below.

Appendix B-1, Church Member Giving, 1968-1996: This table presents data for the denominations which comprise the data set analyzed for the 1968 through 1996 period.

Elements of this data are also used for the analyses in chapters two through six.

In Appendix B-1, the data for the Presbyterian Church (U.S.A.) combined data for the United Presbyterian Church in the U.S.A. and the Presbyterian Church in the United States for the period 1968 through 1982. These two communions merged to become the Presbyterian Church (U.S.A.) in 1983, data for which is presented for 1983 through 1996.

Also in Appendix B-1, data for the Evangelical Lutheran Church in America appears beginning in 1987. Before that, the two major component communions that merged into that new denomination—the American Lutheran Church and the Lutheran Church in America—are listed as individual denominations from 1968 through 1986.

In the Appendix B series, the denomination listed as the Fellowship of Evangelical Bible Churches had been named the Evangelical Mennonite Brethren Church prior to July 1987.

The data for two denominations were obtained as follows.

Data for the American Baptist Churches in the U.S.A. has been obtained directly from the denominational office as follows. In discussions with the American Baptist Churches Office of Planning Resources, it became apparent that there had been no distinction made between the membership of congregations reporting financial data, and total membership for the denomination, when reporting data to the *Yearbook of American and Canadian Churches*. Records were obtained from the denomination for a smaller membership figure that reflected only those congregations reporting financial data. While this revised membership data provided a more useful per member giving figure for Congregational Finances, the total Benevolences figure reported to the *YACC*, while included in the present data set, does reflect contributions to some Benevolences categories from 100% of the American Baptist membership. The membership reported in Appendix B-1 for the American Baptist Churches is the membership for congregations reporting financial data, rather than the total membership figure provided in editions of the *Yearbook of American and Canadian Churches*. However, in the sections that consider membership as a percentage of population, the Total Membership figure for the American Baptist Churches is used.

Appendix B-2, Church Member Giving, 1995-1996: Appendix B-2 presents the Full or Confirmed Membership, Congregational Finances and Benevolences data for the sixteen additional denominations included in the 1995-1996 comparison.

Appendix B-3, Church Member Giving for Eleven Denominations, 1921-1996: This appendix presents additional data which is not included in Appendix B-1 for the Eleven Denominations.

The data from 1921 through 1928 in Appendix B-3.1 is taken from summary information contained in the *Yearbook of American Churches, 1949 Edition*, George F. Ketcham, ed. (Lebanon, PA: Sowers Printing Company,

1949, p. 162). The summary membership data provided is for Inclusive Membership. Therefore, giving as a percentage of income for the years 1921 through 1928 may have been somewhat higher had Full or Confirmed Membership been used. The list of denominations that are summarized for this period is presented in the *Yearbook of American Churches, 1953 Edition*, Benson Y. Landis, ed. (New York: National Council of the Churches of Christ in the U.S.A., 1953, p. 274).

The data from 1929 through 1952 is taken from summary information presented in the *Yearbook of American Churches, Edition for 1955*, Benson Y. Landis, ed. (New York: National Council of the Churches of Christ in the U.S.A., 1954, pp. 286-287). A description of the list of denominations included in the 1929 through 1952 data summary on page 275 of the *YACC Edition for 1955* indicated that the Moravian Church, Northern Province is not included in the 1929 through 1952 data.

The data in Appendix B-3.2 for 1953 through 1964 was obtained for the indicated denominations from the relevant edition of the *YACC* series. Giving as a percentage of income was derived for these years by dividing the published Total Contributions figure by the published Per Capita figure to produce a membership figure for each denomination. The Total Contributions figures for the denominations were added to produce an aggregated Total Contributions figure. The calculated membership figures were also added to produce an aggregated membership figure. The aggregated Total Contributions figure was then divided by the aggregated membership figure to yield a per member giving figure which was used in calculating giving as a percentage of income.

Data for the years 1965 through 1967 was not available in a form that could be readily analyzed for the present purposes, and therefore data for these three years was estimated by dividing the change in per capita Total Contributions from 1964 to 1968 by four, the number of years in this interval, and cumulatively adding the result to the base year of 1964 and the succeeding years of 1965 and 1966 to obtain estimates for the years 1965 through 1967.

In most cases, this procedure was also applied to individual denominations to avoid an artificially low total due to missing data. If data was not available for a specific year, the otherwise blank entry was filled in with a calculation based on surrounding years for that denomination. For example, this procedure was used for the American Baptist Churches for the years 1955 and 1956, the Christian Church (Disciples of Christ) for the years 1955 and 1959, and the Evangelical United Brethren, later to merge into The United Methodist Church, for the years 1957, 1958 and 1959. Data for the Methodist Church was changed for 1957 in a similar manner.

Available Total Contributions and Full or Confirmed Members data for The Episcopal Church and The United Methodist Church for 1969 through 1996 is presented in Appendix B-3.3. These two communions are included in the Eleven Denominations. The United Methodist Church was created in 1968 when The Methodist Church and The Evangelical United Brethren Church merged. While The Methodist Church filed summary data for the year 1968, The Evangelical United Brethren Church did not. Data for these denominations was calculated as noted in the appendix. However, since the 1968 data for The Methodist Church would not have been comparable to the 1985 and 1995 data for The United Methodist Church, this communion was not included in the more focused 1968-1996 analysis.

Appendix B-1: Church Member Giving 1968-1996

Key to Denominational Abbreviations: Data Years 1968-1996

Abbreviation	Denomination
abc	American Baptist Churches in the U.S.A.
alc	The American Lutheran Church
arp	Associate Reformed Presbyterian Church (General Synod)
bcc	Brethren in Christ Church
ccd	Christian Church (Disciples of Christ)
cga	Church of God (Anderson, IN)
cgg	Church of God General Conference (Oregon, IL)
chb	Church of the Brethren
chn	Church of the Nazarene
ccc	Conservative Congregational Christian Conference
cpc	Cumberland Presbyterian Church
ecc	Evangelical Congregational Church
ecv	Evangelical Covenant Church
elc	Evangelical Lutheran Church in America
els	Evangelical Lutheran Synod
emc	Evangelical Mennonite Church
feb	Fellowship of Evangelical Bible Churches
fmc	Free Methodist Church of North America
fum	Friends United Meeting
ggb	General Association of General Baptists
lca	Lutheran Church in America
lms	Lutheran Church-Missouri Synod
mch	Mennonite Church
mca	Moravian Church in America, Northern Province
nab	North American Baptist Conference
opc	The Orthodox Presbyterian Church
pch	Presbyterian Church (U.S.A.)
rca	Reformed Church in America
sda	Seventh-day Adventists
sbc	Southern Baptist Convention
ucc	United Church of Christ
wel	Wisconsin Evangelical Lutheran Synod

Appendix B-1: Church Member Giving, 1968-1996 (continued)

	Data Year 1968			Data Year 1969			Data Year 1970		
	Full/Confirmed Members	Congregational Finances	Benevolences	Full/Confirmed Members	Congregational Finances	Benevolences	Full/Confirmed Members	Congregational Finances	Benevolences
abc	1,179,848 a	95,878,267 a	21,674,924 a	1,153,785 a	104,084,322	21,111,333	1,231,944 a	112,668,310	19,655,391
alc	1,767,618	137,260,390	32,862,410	1,771,999	143,917,440	34,394,570	1,775,573	146,268,320	30,750,030
arp	28,312 a	2,211,002 a	898,430 a	28,273	2,436,936 a	824,628 a	28,427 a	2,585,974 a	806,071 a
bcc	8,954	1,645,256	633,200 a	9,145	1,795,859	817,445	NA	NA	NA
ccd	994,683	105,803,222	21,703,947	936,931	91,169,842	18,946,815	911,964	98,671,692	17,386,032
cga	146,807	23,310,682	4,168,580	147,752	24,828,448	4,531,678	150,198	26,962,037	4,886,223
cgg	6,600	805,000	103,000	6,700	805,000	104,000	6,800	810,000	107,000
chb	187,957	12,975,829	4,889,727	185,198	13,964,158	4,921,991	182,614	14,327,896	4,891,618
chn	364,789	59,943,750 a	14,163,761 a	372,943	64,487,669 a	15,220,339 a	383,284	68,877,922 a	16,221,123 a
ccc	15,127	1,867,978	753,686	16,219	1,382,195	801,534	17,328	1,736,818	779,696
cpc	86,729 a	5,542,678 a	906,583 a	88,091	6,393,665	1,020,248	NA	NA	NA
ecc	29,582 a	3,369,308 a	627,731 a	29,652 a	3,521,074 a	646,187 a	29,437 a	3,786,288 a	692,428 a
ecv	66,021	11,923,084	3,072,848	67,522	12,168,837	3,312,306	67,441	13,309,618	3,578,876
elc	ALC & LCA	ALC & LCA	ALC & LCA	ALC & LCA	ALC & LCA	ALC & LCA	ALC & LCA	ALC & LCA	ALC & LCA
els	10,886 a	844,235 a	241,949 a	11,079	1,003,746	315,325	11,030	969,625	242,831 a
emc	2,870 a	447,397	232,331	NA	NA	NA	NA	NA	NA
feb	1,712 a	156,789 a	129,818 a	3,324	389,000	328,000	3,698	381,877	706,398
fmc	47,831 a	12,032,016 a	2,269,677 a	47,954 a	9,152,729	7,495,653	64,901	9,641,202	7,985,264
fum	55,469	3,564,793	1,256,192	55,257	3,509,509	1,289,026	53,970	3,973,802	1,167,183
ggb	65,000	4,303,183 a	269,921 a	NA	NA	NA	NA	NA	NA
lca	2,279,383	166,337,149	39,981,858	2,193,321	161,958,669	46,902,225	2,187,015	169,795,380	42,118,870
lms	1,877,799	178,042,762	47,415,800	1,900,708	185,827,626	49,402,590	1,922,569	193,352,322	47,810,664
mch	85,682 a	7,078,164 a	5,576,305 a	85,343	7,398,182	6,038,730	83,747 a	7,980,917 a	6,519,476 a
mca	27,772	2,583,354	444,910	27,617	2,642,529	456,182	27,173	2,704,105	463,219
nab	42,371 a	5,176,669 a	1,383,964 a	55,100	6,681,410	2,111,588	55,080	6,586,929	2,368,288
opc	9,197	1,638,437	418,102	9,276	1,761,242	464,660	NA	NA	NA
pch	4,180,093	375,248,474	102,622,450	4,118,664	388,268,169	97,897,522	4,041,813	401,785,731	93,927,852
rca	226,819 a	25,410,489 a	9,197,642 a	224,992 a	27,139,579 a	9,173,312 a	223,353 a	29,421,849 a	9,479,503 a
sda	395,159 a	36,976,280	95,178,335	407,766	40,378,426	102,730,594	420,419	45,280,059	109,569,241
sbc	11,332,229 a	666,924,020 a	128,023,731 a	11,487,708	709,246,590	133,203,885	11,628,032	753,510,973	138,480,329
ucc	2,032,648 a	152,301,536	18,869,136	1,997,898	152,791,512	27,338,543	1,960,608	155,248,767	26,934,289
wel	259,954 a	19,000,023 a	6,574,308 a	265,069	20,786,613	6,417,042	271,117	22,582,545	6,810,612
Total	27,815,901	2,120,602,216	566,545,256	27,705,286	2,189,890,976	598,217,951	27,739,535	2,293,220,958	594,338,507

a Data obtained from denominational source.
Note: Data in italics indicates a change from the previous edition in the series.

Appendix B-1: Church Member Giving, 1968-1996 (continued)

	Data Year 1971			Data Year 1972			Data Year 1973		
	Full/Confirmed Members	Congregational Finances	Benevolences	Full/Confirmed Members	Congregational Finances	Benevolences	Full/Confirmed Members	Congregational Finances	Benevolences
abc	1,223,735 a	114,673,805	18,878,769	1,176,092 a	118,446,573	18,993,440	1,190,455 a	139,357,611 a	20,537,388
alc	1,775,774	146,324,460	28,321,740	1,773,414	154,786,570	30,133,850	1,770,119	168,194,730	35,211,440
arp	28,443 a	2,942,577 a	814,703 a	28,711 a	3,329,446 a	847,665 a	28,763 a	3,742,773 a	750,387 a
bcc	9,550	2,357,786	851,725	9,730	2,440,400	978,957	NA	NA	NA
ccd	884,929	94,091,862	17,770,799	881,467	105,763,511	18,323,685	868,895	112,526,538	19,800,843
cga	152,787	28,343,604	5,062,282	155,920	31,580,751	5,550,487	157,828	34,649,592	6,349,695
ogg	7,200	860,000	120,000	7,400	900,000	120,000	7,440	940,000	120,000
chb	181,183	14,535,274	5,184,768	179,641	14,622,319 b	5,337,277 b	179,333	16,474,758	6,868,927
chn	394,197	75,107,918 a	17,859,332 a	404,732	82,891,903 a	20,119,679 a	417,200	91,318,469 a	22,661,140 a
ccc	19,279 a	1,875,010 a	930,485 a	20,081 a	1,950,865 a	994,453 a	20,712 a	2,080,038 a	1,057,869 a
cpc	57,147	6,848,115	1,139,480	56,212	8,449,593	554,843	56,584	9,715,351	847,727
ecc	29,682 a	4,076,576 a	742,293 a	29,434 a	4,303,406 a	798,968 a	29,331 a	4,913,214 a	943,619 a
ecv	68,428	14,857,190	3,841,887	69,815	14,557,206	4,169,053	69,922	15,500,129	4,259,950
elc	ALC & LCA	ALC & LCA	ALC & LCA	ALC & LCA	ALC & LCA	ALC & LCA	ALC & LCA	ALC & LCA	ALC & LCA
els	11,426 a	1,067,650 a	314,335 a	11,532	1,138,953	295,941 a	12,525	1,296,326	330,052 a
emc	NA	NA	NA	NA	NA	NA	3,131	593,070	408,440
feb	NA	NA	NA	NA	NA	NA	NA	NA	NA
fmc	65,040	13,863,601	6,092,503	48,455	15,206,381	6,638,789	48,763 a	17,483,258	7,000,353
fum	54,522	3,888,064	1,208,062	54,927	4,515,463	1,297,088	57,690	5,037,848	1,327,439
ggb	NA	NA	NA	NA	NA	NA	NA	NA	NA
lca	2,175,378	179,570,467	43,599,913	2,165,591	188,387,949	45,587,481	2,169,341	200,278,486	34,627,978
lms	1,945,889	203,619,804	48,891,368	1,963,262	216,756,345	50,777,670	1,983,114	230,435,598	54,438,074
mch	88,522	8,171,316	7,035,750	89,505	9,913,176	7,168,664	90,967	9,072,858	6,159,740
mca	26,101	2,576,172	459,447	25,500	2,909,252	465,316	25,468	3,020,667	512,424
nab	54,997	7,114,457	2,293,692	54,441	7,519,558	2,253,158	41,516	6,030,352	1,712,092
opc	NA	NA	NA	NA	NA	NA	NA	NA	NA
pch	3,963,665	420,865,807	93,164,548	3,855,494	436,042,890	92,691,469	3,730,312 c	480,735,088 c	95,462,247 c
rca	219,915 a	32,217,319 a	9,449,655 a	217,583 a	34,569,874 a	9,508,818 a	212,906 a	39,524,443 a	10,388,619 a
sda	433,906	49,208,043	119,913,879	449,188	54,988,781	132,411,980	464,276	60,643,602	149,994,942
sbc	11,824,676	814,406,626	160,510,775	12,065,333	896,427,208	174,711,648	12,295,400	1,011,467,569	193,511,983
ucc	1,928,674	158,924,956	26,409,521	1,895,016	165,556,364	27,793,561	1,867,810	168,602,602	28,471,058
wel	275,500	24,365,692	7,481,644	278,442	26,649,585	8,232,320	283,130	29,450,094	8,650,699
Total	27,900,545	2,426,754,151	628,343,355	27,966,918	2,604,604,322	666,756,260	28,082,931	2,863,085,064	712,405,125

[a] Data obtained from denominational source.

[b] YACC Church of the Brethren figures reported for 15 months due to fiscal year change; adjusted here to 12/15ths.

[c] The Presbyterian Church (USA) data for 1973 combines United Presbyterian Church in the U.S.A. data for 1973 (see YACC 1975) and an average of Presbyterian Church in the United States data for 1972 and 1974, since 1973 data was not reported in the YACC series.

Note: Data in italics indicates a change from the previous edition in the series.

Appendix B-1: Church Member Giving, 1968-1996 (continued)

	Data Year 1974			Data Year 1975			Data Year 1976		
	Full/Confirmed Members	Congregational Finances	Benevolences	Full/Confirmed Members	Congregational Finances	Benevolences	Full/Confirmed Members	Congregational Finances	Benevolences
abc	1,176,989 a	147,022,280	21,847,285	1,180,793 a	153,697,091	23,638,372	1,142,773 a	163,134,092	25,792,357
alc	1,764,186	173,318,574	38,921,546	1,764,810	198,863,519	75,666,809	1,768,758	215,527,544	76,478,278
arp	28,570	3,935,533 a	868,284 a	28,589	4,820,846 a	929,880 a	28,581	5,034,270 a	1,018,913 a
bcc	10,255	3,002,218	1,078,576	10,784	3,495,152	955,845	11,375	4,088,492	1,038,484
ccd	854,844	119,434,435	20,818,434	859,885	126,553,931	22,126,459	845,058	135,008,269	23,812,274
cga	161,401	39,189,287	7,343,123	166,259	42,077,029	7,880,559	170,285	47,191,302	8,854,295
cgg	7,455	975,000	105,000	7,485	990,000	105,000	7,620	1,100,000	105,000
chb	179,387	18,609,614	7,281,551	179,336	20,338,351	7,842,819 b	178,157	22,133,858	8,032,293
chn	430,128	104,774,391	25,534,267 a	441,093	115,400,881	28,186,392 a	448,658	128,294,499	32,278,187 a
ccc	21,661 a	2,452,254 a	1,181,655 a	22,065 a	2,639,472 a	1,750,364 a	21,703 a	3,073,413 a	1,494,355 a
cpc	55,577	9,619,526	1,087,680	90,005	11,392,729	1,215,279	88,382	10,919,882	1,648,770
ecc	29,636 a	4,901,100 a	1,009,726 a	28,886 a	5,503,484 a	1,068,134 a	28,840 a	6,006,621 a	1,139,209 a
ecv	69,960	17,044,074	5,131,124	71,808	19,875,977	6,353,422	73,458	21,451,544	6,898,871
elc	ALC & LCA	ALC & LCA	ALC & LCA	ALC & LCA	ALC & LCA	ALC & LCA	ALC & LCA	ALC & LCA	ALC & LCA
els	13,097	1,519,749	411,732 a	13,489 a	1,739,255	438,875 a	14,504	2,114,998	521,018 a
emc	3,123	644,548	548,000	NA	NA	NA	3,350	800,000	628,944
feb	NA	NA	NA	NA	NA	NA	NA	NA	NA
fmc	49,314 a	16,734,865	7,373,664	50,632	18,336,422	8,143,838	51,565	19,954,186	9,261,347
fum	NA	NA	NA	56,605	6,428,458	1,551,036	51,032	6,749,045	1,691,190
ggb	NA	NA	NA	NA	NA	NA	NA	NA	NA
lca	2,166,615	228,081,405	44,531,126	2,183,131	222,637,156	55,646,303	2,187,995	243,449,466	58,761,005
lms	2,010,456	249,150,470	55,076,955	2,018,530	266,546,758	55,896,061	2,026,336	287,098,403	56,831,860
mch	92,930 a	13,792,266	9,887,051	94,209	15,332,908	11,860,385	96,092 a	17,215,234	12,259,924
mca	25,583	3,304,388	513,685	25,512	3,567,406	552,512	24,938	4,088,195	573,619
nab	41,437	6,604,693	2,142,148	42,122	7,781,298	2,470,317	42,277	8,902,540	3,302,348
opc	NA	NA	NA	NA	NA	NA	10,372	3,287,612	892,889
pch	3,619,768	502,237,350	100,966,089	3,535,825	529,327,006	111,027,318	3,484,985	563,106,353	125,035,379
rca	210,866 a	41,053,364 a	11,470,631 a	212,349 a	44,681,053	11,994,379 a	211,628 a	49,083,734 a	13,163,739 a
sda	479,799	67,241,956	166,166,766	495,699	72,060,121	184,689,250	509,792	81,577,130	184,648,454
sbc	12,513,378	1,123,264,849	219,214,770	12,733,124	1,237,594,037	237,452,055	12,917,992	1,382,794,494	262,144,889
ucc	1,841,312	184,292,017	30,243,223	1,818,762	193,524,114	32,125,332	1,801,241	207,486,324	33,862,658
wel	286,858	32,683,492	10,002,869	293,237	35,889,331	11,212,937	297,862	40,017,991	11,300,102
Total	28,144,585	3,114,883,698	790,756,960	28,425,024	3,361,093,785	902,779,932	28,545,609	3,680,689,491	963,470,651

[a]Data obtained from denominational source.

[b]YACC Church of the Brethren figures reported for 15 months due to fiscal year change; adjusted here to 12/15ths.

Note: Data in italics indicates a change from the previous edition in the series.

Appendix B-1: Church Member Giving, 1968-1996 (continued)

	Data Year 1977			Data Year 1978			Data Year 1979		
	Full/Confirmed Members	Congregational Finances	Benevolences	Full/Confirmed Members	Congregational Finances	Benevolences	Full/Confirmed Members	Congregational Finances	Benevolences
abc	1,146,084 a	172,710,063	27,765,800	1,008,495 a	184,716,172	31,937,862	1,036,054 a	195,986,995	34,992,300
alc	1,772,227	231,960,304	54,085,201	1,773,179	256,371,804	57,145,861	1,768,071	284,019,905	63,903,906
arp	28,371 a	5,705,295 a	1,061,285 a	28,644	6,209,447 a	1,031,469 a	28,513	6,544,759 a	1,125,562 a
bcc	NA	NA	NA	NA	NA	NA	12,923	5,519,037	1,312,046
ccd	817,288	148,880,340	25,698,856	791,633	166,249,455	25,790,367	773,765	172,270,978	27,335,440
cga	171,947	51,969,150	10,001,062	173,753	57,630,848	11,214,530	175,113	65,974,517	12,434,621
cgg	7,595	1,130,000	110,000	7,550	1,135,000	110,000	7,620	1,170,000	105,000
chb	177,534	23,722,817	8,228,903	175,335	25,397,531	9,476,220	172,115	28,422,684	10,161,266
chn	455,100	141,807,024	34,895,751 a	462,124	153,943,138	38,300,431 a	473,726	170,515,940 a	42,087,862 a
ccc	21,897 a	3,916,248 a	1,554,143 a	22,364 a	4,271,435 a	1,630,565 a	23,481 a	4,969,610 a	1,871,754 a
cpc	88,353	11,611,365	1,781,862	88,093	13,657,931	2,136,706	89,218	13,905,745	2,513,625
ecc	28,712 a	6,356,730 a	1,277,310 a	28,459 a	6,890,381 a	1,454,826 a	27,995 a	7,552,495 a	1,547,857 a
ecv	74,060	23,531,176	7,240,548	74,678	26,200,708	8,017,623	76,092	29,987,284	9,400,074
elc	ALC & LCA	ALC & LCA	ALC & LCA	ALC & LCA	ALC & LCA	ALC & LCA	ALC & LCA	ALC & LCA	ALC & LCA
els	14,652	2,290,697	546,899 a	14,833	2,629,719	833,543 a	15,081	2,750,703	904,774 a
emc	NA	NA	NA	3,634	1,281,761	794,896	3,704	1,380,806	828,264
feb	NA	NA	NA	3,956	970,960	745,059	NA	NA	NA
fmc	52,563	22,417,964	10,163,648	55,493	23,911,458	10,121,800	NA	NA	NA
fum	52,599	6,943,990	1,895,984	53,390	8,172,337	1,968,884	51,426	6,662,787	2,131,108
ggb	72,030	9,854,533	747,842	NA	NA	NA	73,046	13,131,345	1,218,763
lca	2,191,942	251,083,883	62,076,894	2,183,666	277,186,563	72,426,148	2,177,231	301,605,382	71,325,097
lms	1,991,408	301,064,630	57,077,162	1,969,279	329,134,237	59,030,753	1,965,422	360,989,735	63,530,596
mch	96,609	18,540,237	12,980,502	97,142	22,922,417	14,124,757 a	98,027	24,505,346	15,116,762
mca	25,323	4,583,616	581,200	24,854	4,441,750	625,536	24,782	4,600,331	689,070
nab	42,724	10,332,556	3,554,204	42,499	11,629,309	3,559,983	42,779	13,415,024	3,564,339
opc	10,920	3,514,172	931,935	10,939	4,107,705	1,135,388	11,300	4,683,302	1,147,191
pch	3,430,927	633,187,916	130,252,348	3,382,783	692,872,811	128,194,954	3,321,787	776,049,247	148,528,993
rca	210,637 a	53,999,791 a	14,210,966 a	211,778 a	60,138,720 a	15,494,816 a	210,700 a	62,997,526 a	16,750,408 a
sda	522,317	98,468,365	216,202,975	535,705	104,044,989	226,692,736	553,089	118,711,906	255,936,372
sbc	13,078,239	1,506,877,921	289,179,711	13,191,394	1,668,120,760	316,462,385	13,372,757	1,864,213,869	355,885,769
ucc	1,785,652	219,878,772	35,522,221	1,769,104	232,593,033	37,789,958	1,745,533	249,443,032	41,100,583
wel	301,944	44,492,259	11,639,834	303,944	50,255,539	12,960,885	306,264	54,983,467	14,230,208
Total	28,669,654	4,010,831,814	1,021,259,046	28,488,700	4,397,087,918	1,091,208,941	28,637,614	4,846,963,757	1,201,679,610

aData obtained from denominational source.
Note: Data in italics indicates a change from the previous edition in the series.

Appendix B-1: Church Member Giving, 1968-1996 (continued)

	Data Year 1980			Data Year 1981			Data Year 1982		
	Full/Confirmed Members	Congregational Finances	Benevolences	Full/Confirmed Members	Congregational Finances	Benevolences	Full/Confirmed Members	Congregational Finances	Benevolences
abc	1,008,700 a	213,560,656	37,133,159	989,322 a	227,931,461	40,046,261	983,580 a	242,750,027	41,457,745
alc	1,763,067	312,592,610	65,235,739	1,758,452	330,155,588	96,102,638	1,758,239	359,848,865	77,010,444
arp	28,166 a	6,868,650 a	1,054,229 a	28,334 a	7,863,221 a	1,497,838 a	29,087 a	8,580,311 a	1,807,572 a
bcc	NA	NA	NA	13,993	6,781,857	1,740,711	NA	NA	NA
ccd	788,394	189,176,399	30,991,519	772,466	211,828,751	31,067,142	770,227	227,178,861	34,307,638
cga	176,429	67,367,485	13,414,112	178,581	78,322,907	14,907,277	184,685	84,896,806	17,171,600
cgg	NA	NA	NA	5,981	1,788,298	403,000	NA	NA	NA
chb	170,839	29,813,265	11,663,976	170,267	31,641,019	12,929,076	168,844	35,064,568	12,844,415
chn	483,101	191,536,556	45,786,446 a	490,852	203,145,992	50,084,163 a	497,261	221,947,940	53,232,461 a
ccc	24,410 a	6,017,539 a	2,169,298 a	25,044 a	8,465,804	2,415,233	26,008	9,230,111	2,574,569
cpc	90,844	16,448,164	2,835,695	91,665	17,225,308	3,504,763	91,774	18,600,022	2,703,521
ecc	27,567 a	8,037,564 a	1,630,993 a	27,287 a	8,573,057 a	1,758,025 a	27,203 a	9,119,278 a	1,891,936 a
ecv	77,737	33,191,322	10,031,072	79,523	37,884,792	8,689,918	81,324	42,599,609	8,830,793
elc	ALC & LCA	ALC & LCA	ALC & LCA	ALC & LCA	ALC & LCA	ALC & LCA	ALC & LCA	ALC & LCA	ALC & LCA
els	14,968	3,154,804	876,929 a	14,904	3,461,387	716,624	15,165	3,767,977	804,822
emc	3,782	1,527,945	1,041,447	3,753	1,515,975	908,342	3,832	1,985,890	731,510
feb	4,329	1,250,466	627,536	NA	NA	NA	2,047	696,660	1,020,972
fmc	NA	NA	NA	NA	NA	NA	54,198	35,056,434	8,051,593
fum	51,691	9,437,724	2,328,137	51,248	9,551,765	2,449,731	50,601	10,334,180	2,597,215
ggb	74,159	14,967,312	1,547,038	75,028	15,816,060	1,473,070	NA	NA	NA
lca	2,176,991	371,981,816	87,439,137	2,173,558	404,300,509	82,862,299	2,176,265	435,564,519	83,217,264
lms	1,973,958	390,756,268	66,626,364	1,983,198	429,910,406	86,341,102	1,961,260	468,468,156	75,457,846
mch	99,511	28,846,931	16,437,738	99,651	31,304,278	17,448,024	101,501	33,583,338	17,981,274
mca	24,863	5,178,444	860,399	24,500	5,675,495	831,177	24,669	6,049,857	812,015
nab	43,041	12,453,858	3,972,485	43,146	15,513,286	4,420,403	42,735	17,302,952	4,597,515
opc	11,550	5,235,294	1,235,849	11,889	5,939,983	1,382,451	NA	NA	NA
pch	3,262,086	820,218,732	176,172,729	3,202,392	896,641,430	188,576,382	3,157,372	970,223,947	199,331,832
rca	210,762	70,733,297	17,313,239 a	210,312	77,044,709	18,193,793 a	211,168	82,656,050	19,418,165 a
sda	571,141	121,484,768	275,783,385	588,536	133,088,131	297,838,046	606,310	136,877,455	299,437,917
sbc	13,600,126	2,080,375,258	400,976,072	13,782,644	2,336,062,506	443,931,179	13,991,709	2,628,272,553	486,402,607
ucc	1,736,244	278,546,571	44,042,186	1,726,535	300,730,591	48,329,399	1,708,847	323,725,191	52,738,069
wel	308,620	60,624,862	16,037,844	311,351	68,056,396	18,261,099	312,195	71,891,457 a	18,677,343
Total	28,807,076	5,351,384,560	1,335,264,752	28,934,412	5,906,220,962	1,479,109,166	29,038,106	6,486,273,014	1,525,110,653

[a]Data obtained from denominational source.
Note: Data in italics indicates a change from the previous edition in the series.

Appendix B-1: Church Member Giving, 1968-1996 (continued)

	Data Year 1983			Data Year 1984			Data Year 1985		
	Full/Confirmed Members	Congregational Finances	Benevolences	Full/Confirmed Members	Congregational Finances	Benevolences	Full/Confirmed Members	Congregational Finances	Benevolences
abc	965,117 a	254,716,036	43,683,021	953,945 a	267,556,088	46,232,040	894,732 a	267,694,684	47,201,119
alc	1,756,420	375,500,188	84,633,617	1,756,558	413,876,101	86,601,067	1,751,649	428,861,660	87,152,699
arp	31,738	10,640,050 a	2,180,230 a	31,355	11,221,526 a	3,019,456 a	32,051	12,092,868 a	3,106,994 a
bcc	14,782	7,638,413	1,858,632	15,128	8,160,359	2,586,843	15,535 a	8,504,354 a	2,979,046 a
ocd	761,629	241,934,972	35,809,331	755,233	263,694,210	38,402,791	743,486	274,072,301	40,992,053
oga	182,190	81,309,323	13,896,753	185,404	86,611,269	14,347,570	185,593	91,078,512	15,308,954
ogg	5,759	1,981,300	412,000	4,711	2,211,800	504,200	4,575	2,428,730	582,411
chb	164,680	39,726,743	14,488,192	161,824	37,743,527	15,136,600	159,184	40,658,904	16,509,718
chn	506,439	237,220,642	57,267,073 a	514,937	253,566,280	60,909,810 a	520,741	267,134,078	65,627,515 a
ccc	26,691 a	9,189,221 a	2,980,636	28,383	10,018,982	3,051,425	28,624	11,729,365	3,350,021
cpc	93,387	20,206,646	2,604,569	92,242	21,185,481	3,843,056	85,346 a	21,241,302 a	3,227,932 a
ecc	26,769 a	9,505,479 a	2,019,373 a	26,375 a	10,302,554 a	2,220,852 a	26,016	8,134,641 a	1,777,172
ecv	82,943	46,397,734	10,615,909	84,185	51,613,393	11,243,908	85,150	54,719,309	13,828,030
elc	ALC & LCA	ALC & LCA	ALC & LCA	ALC & LCA	ALC & LCA	ALC & LCA	ALC & LCA	ALC & LCA	ALC & LCA
els	15,576	3,842,625	838,788	15,396	4,647,714	931,677 a	15,012	4,725,783	791,586
emc	3,857	1,930,689	738,194	3,908	2,017,565	862,350	3,813	2,128,019	1,058,040
feb	2,094	622,467	1,466,399	NA	NA	NA	2,107 a	1,069,851 a	402,611 a
fmc	NA	NA	NA	NA	NA	NA	56,242	42,046,626 a	9,461,369 a
fum	49,441	11,723,240	2,886,931	48,713	11,549,163	2,875,370	48,812	12,601,820	3,012,658
ggb	75,133	17,283,259	1,733,755	75,028	17,599,169	1,729,228	73,040	18,516,252	1,683,130
lca	2,176,772	457,239,780	88,909,363	2,168,594	496,228,216	99,833,067	2,161,216	539,142,069	103,534,375
lms	1,984,199	499,220,552	97,293,050	1,986,392	539,346,935	104,393,798	1,982,753	566,507,516	105,191,123
mch	103,350 a	34,153,628	17,581,878	90,347	37,333,306	16,944,094	91,167	34,015,200	25,593,500
mca	24,913	6,618,339	911,787	24,269	7,723,611	1,183,741	24,396	8,698,949	1,170,349
nab	43,286	18,010,853	5,132,672	43,215	19,322,720	5,724,552	42,863	20,246,236	5,766,686
opc	12,045	6,874,722	1,755,169	12,239	7,555,006	2,079,924	12,634	8,291,483	2,204,998
pch	3,122,213	1,047,756,995	197,981,080	3,092,151	1,132,098,779	218,412,639	3,057,226 a	1,252,885,684	232,487,569 a
rca	211,660	92,071,986	20,632,574	209,968 a	100,378,778	21,794,880	209,395	103,428,950	22,233,299
sda	623,563	143,636,140	323,461,439	638,929	155,257,063	319,664,449	651,594	155,077,180	346,251,406
sbc	14,178,051	2,838,573,815	528,781,000	14,341,822	3,094,913,877	567,467,188	14,477,364	3,272,276,486	609,868,694
ucc	1,701,513	332,613,396	55,716,557	1,696,107	385,786,198	58,679,094	1,683,777	409,543,989	62,169,679 a
wel	313,883	76,133,614 a	24,169,441	315,466	82,884,471 a	22,951,699	316,297 a	87,194,889 a	22,376,423 a
Total	29,260,093	6,924,272,847	1,642,439,413	29,372,824	7,532,404,141	1,733,627,368	29,442,390	8,026,747,690	1,856,901,159

[a]Data obtained from denominational source.
Note: Data in italics indicates a change from the previous edition in the series.

Appendix B-1: Church Member Giving, 1968-1996 (continued)

	Data Year 1986			Data Year 1987			Data Year 1988		
	Full/Confirmed Members	Congregational Finances	Benevolences	Full/Confirmed Members	Congregational Finances	Benevolences	Full/Confirmed Members	Congregational Finances	Benevolences
abc	862,582 a	287,020,378 a	49,070,083 a	868,189 a	291,606,418 a	55,613,855	825,102 a	296,569,316 d	55,876,771
alc	1,740,439	434,641,736	96,147,129	See ELCA	See ELCA	See ELCA	See ELCA	See ELCA	See ELCA
arp	32,438 a	12,336,321 a	3,434,408 a	32,289	13,553,176 a	3,927,030 a	31,922	13,657,776 a	5,063,036 a
bcc	15,911	10,533,883	2,463,558	16,136	11,203,321	3,139,949	NA	NA	NA
ccd	732,466	288,277,386	42,027,504	718,522	287,464,332	42,728,826	707,985	297,187,996	42,226,128
oga	188,662	91,768,855	16,136,647	198,552	124,376,413	20,261,687	198,842	132,384,232	19,781,941
ogg	NA	NA	NA	4,348	2,437,778	738,818	NA	NA	NA
chb	155,967	43,531,293	17,859,101	154,067	45,201,732	19,342,402	151,169	48,008,657	19,701,942 a
chn	529,192	283,189,977	68,438,998 a	541,878	294,160,356	73,033,568 a	550,700	309,478,442	74,737,057 a
ccc	28,948	15,559,846 a	3,961,037	29,429	15,409,349 a	3,740,688	29,015	13,853,547	4,120,974
cpc	91,556	22,992,625	3,782,282	85,781	22,857,711	3,727,681	85,304	23,366,911 d	3,722,607
ecc	25,625	10,977,813 a	2,422,879 a	25,300	14,281,140 a	2,575,415 a	24,980	12,115,762	2,856,766 a
ecv	86,079	57,628,572	14,374,707	86,741	73,498,123 a	14,636,000	87,750	77,504,445 a	14,471,178
elc	ALC & LCA	ALC & LCA	ALC & LCA	3,952,663	1,083,293,684	169,685,942	3,931,878	1,150,483,034	169,580,472
els	15,083 a	4,996,111 a	1,050,715 a	15,892	5,298,882	1,082,198	NA	NA	NA
emc	NA	NA	NA	3,841	2,332,216	1,326,711	3,879	2,522,533	1,438,459
feb	NA	NA	NA	NA	NA	NA	NA	NA	NA
fmc	56,243	46,150,881	9,446,120	57,262	47,743,298	9,938,096	57,432	48,788,041	9,952,103
fum	48,143	12,790,909	2,916,870	47,173	13,768,272	3,631,353	48,325	14,127,491	3,719,125
ggb	72,263	19,743,265	1,883,826	73,515	20,850,827	1,789,578	74,086	21,218,051	1,731,299
lca	2,157,701	569,250,519	111,871,174	See ELCA	See ELCA	See ELCA	See ELCA	See ELCA	See ELCA
lms	1,974,798	605,768,688	111,938,197	1,973,347	620,271,274	109,681,025	1,962,674	659,288,332	112,694,841
mch	91,467 a	40,097,500 a	24,404,200 a	92,673 a	43,295,100	25,033,600	92,682	47,771,200	27,043,900
mca	24,260	8,133,127	1,155,350	24,440	9,590,658	1,174,593	23,526	9,221,646	1,210,476
nab	42,084	20,961,799	5,982,391	NA	NA	NA	42,629	24,597,288	6,611,840
opc	NA	NA	NA	13,301	9,884,288	2,425,480	NA	NA	NA
pch	3,007,322	1,318,440,264	249,033,881	2,967,781	1,395,501,073	247,234,439	2,929,608	1,439,655,217	284,989,138
rca	207,993	114,231,429	22,954,596	203,581	114,652,192 a	24,043,270	200,631	127,409,263	25,496,802 a
sda	666,199	166,692,974	361,316,753	675,702	166,939,355	374,830,065	687,200	178,768,967	395,849,223
sbc	14,613,638	3,481,124,471	635,196,984	14,722,617	3,629,842,643	662,455,177	14,812,844	3,706,652,161	689,366,904
ucc	1,676,105	429,340,239	63,808,091	1,662,568	451,700,210	66,870,922	1,644,787	470,747,740	65,734,348
wel	316,416	92,662,969 a	22,448,920	317,294	97,567,101 a	22,207,123	316,987	101,975,092 a	22,406,238
Total	29,459,580	8,488,843,830	1,945,526,401	29,564,882	8,908,580,922	1,966,875,491	29,521,937	9,227,353,140	2,060,383,568

aData obtained from denominational source.
dA YACC prepublication data table listed 23,366,911 for Congregational Finances which, added to Benevolences, equals the published Total of 27,089,518.
Note: Data in italics indicates a change from the previous edition in the series.

Appendix B-1: Church Member Giving, 1968-1996 (continued)

	Data Year 1989			Data Year 1990			Data Year 1991		
	Full/Confirmed Members	Congregational Finances	Benevolences	Full/Confirmed Members	Congregational Finances	Benevolences	Full/Confirmed Members	Congregational Finances	Benevolences
abc	789,730 a	305,212,094 a	55,951,539	764,890 a	315,777,005 a	54,740,278 a	773,838 a	318,150,548 a	52,330,924 a
alc	See ELCA	See ELCA	See ELCA	See ELCA	See ELCA	See ELCA	See ELCA	See ELCA	See ELCA
arp	32,600	*16,053,762* a	*4,367,314* a	32,817 a	*17,313,355* a	*5,031,504* a	33,494 a	*17,585,273* a	*5,254,738* a
bcc	16,842	12,840,038	3,370,306	17,277	13,327,414	3,336,580	17,456 a	14,491,918 a	3,294,169 a
ccd	690,115	310,043,826	42,015,246	678,750	321,569,909	42,607,007	663,336	331,629,009	43,339,307
cga	199,786	134,918,052	20,215,075	205,884	141,375,027	21,087,504	214,743 a	146,249,447 a	21,801,570 a
ogg	4,415	3,367,000	686,000	4,399	3,106,729	690,000	4,375	2,756,651	662,500
chb	149,681	51,921,820	19,737,714 a	148,253	54,832,226	18,384,483 a	147,954 a	55,035,355 a	19,694,919 a
chn	558,664	322,924,598	76,625,913 a	563,756 a	333,397,255 a	77,991,665 a	572,153	352,654,251	82,276,097 a
ccc	28,413	18,199,823	4,064,111	28,355	16,964,128	4,174,133	28,035	17,760,290	4,304,052
cpc	84,866	25,326,430	4,092,869	91,857	28,364,344	4,355,823	91,650 a	29,442,581 a	5,972,155 a
ecc	24,606	*13,274,756* a	*2,703,095* a	24,437	*12,947,150* a	*2,858,077* a	24,124 a	*13,100,036* a	*3,074,660* a
ecv	89,014	*80,621,293* a	15,206,265	89,735	*84,263,236* a	15,601,475	89,648	87,321,563 a	16,598,656
elc	3,909,302	1,239,433,257	182,386,940 a	3,898,478	1,318,884,279	184,174,554	3,890,947	1,375,439,787	186,016,168
els	15,740	6,186,648	1,342,321	16,181	6,527,076	1,193,789	16,004	6,657,338	1,030,445
emc	3,888	2,712,843	1,567,728	4,026	2,991,485	1,800,593	3,958 a	3,394,563	1,790,115
feb	NA	NA	NA	NA	NA	NA	2,008 a	1,398,968 a	500,092 a
fmc	59,418 a	50,114,090 a	10,311,535 a	58,084	55,229,181	10,118,505	57,794	57,880,464	9,876,739
fum	47,228	16,288,644	4,055,624	45,691	10,036,083	2,511,063	*50,803* e	NA	NA
ggb	73,738	23,127,835	1,768,804	74,156	23,127,835	1,737,011	71,119 a	22,362,874 a	1,408,262 a
lca	See ELCA	See ELCA	See ELCA	See ELCA	See ELCA	See ELCA	See ELCA	See ELCA	See ELCA
lms	1,961,114	701,701,168 a	118,511,582 a	1,954,350	712,235,204	129,229,080	1,952,845	741,823,412	124,932,427
mch	92,517	55,353,313	27,873,241	92,448 a	65,709,827	28,397,083	93,114 a	68,926,324	28,464,199
mca	23,802	10,415,640	1,284,233	23,526	10,105,037	1,337,616	22,887	10,095,337	1,205,335
nab	42,629	28,076,077	3,890,017	44,493	31,103,672	7,700,119	43,187 a	27,335,239 a	7,792,876 a
opc	NA	NA	NA	NA	NA	NA	12,265	11,700,000	2,700,000
pch	2,886,482	1,528,450,805	295,365,032	2,847,437	1,530,341,707	294,990,441	2,805,548	1,636,407,042	311,905,934 a
rca	198,832	136,796,188 a	29,456,132 a	197,154	144,357,953 a	27,705,029 a	193,531 a	147,532,382 a	26,821,721 a
sda	701,781	196,204,538	415,752,350	717,446	195,054,218	433,035,080	733,026	201,411,183	456,242,995
sbc	14,907,826	3,873,300,782	712,738,838	15,038,409	4,146,285,561	718,174,874	15,232,347	4,283,283,059	731,812,766
ucc	1,625,969	496,825,160	72,300,698	1,599,212	527,378,397	71,984,897	1,583,830	543,803,752	73,149,887
wel	317,117	110,575,539 a	22,811,571	316,813	116,272,092 a	24,088,568	316,929 a	121,835,547 a	24,276,370 a
Total	29,536,115	9,770,266,019	2,150,452,093	29,578,314	10,238,877,385	2,189,036,831	29,692,145	10,647,464,193	2,248,530,078

[a] Data obtained from denominational source.
[e] Inclusive membership used only in Chapter 5 analysis.
Note: Data in italics indicates a change from the previous edition in the series.

91

Appendix B-1: Church Member Giving, 1968-1996 (continued)

	Data Year 1992			Data Year 1993			Data Year 1994		
	Full/Confirmed Members	Congregational Finances	Benevolences	Full/Confirmed Members	Congregational Finances	Benevolences	Full/Confirmed Members	Congregational Finances	Benevolences
abc	730,009 a	310,307,040 a	52,764,005	764,657 a	346,658,047 a	53,562,811	697,379 a	337,185,885 a	51,553,256 a
alc	See ELCA	See ELCA	See ELCA	See ELCA	See ELCA	See ELCA	See ELCA	See ELCA	See ELCA
arp	33,550	18,175,957 a	5,684,008 a	33,662 a	20,212,390 a	5,822,845 a	33,636	22,618,802 a	6,727,857
bcc	17,646 a	15,981,118 a	3,159,717 a	17,986	13,786,394	4,515,730 a	18,152	14,844,672	5,622,005
ccd	655,652	333,629,412	46,440,333	619,028	328,219,027	44,790,415	605,996	342,352,080	43,165,285
oga	214,743	150,115,497	23,500,213	216,117	158,454,703	23,620,177	221,346 a	160,694,760 a	26,262,049 a
ogg	4,085	2,648,085	509,398	4,239	2,793,000	587,705	3,996	2,934,843	475,799
chb	147,912	57,954,895	21,748,320	146,713	56,818,998	23,278,848	144,282	57,210,682	24,155,595
chn	582,804 a	361,555,793 a	84,118,580 a	589,398	369,896,767	87,416,378 a	595,303	387,385,034	89,721,860
ccc	30,387	22,979,946	4,311,234	36,864	24,997,736 a	5,272,184	37,996 a	23,758,101 a	5,240,805 a
cpc	92,240	29,721,914	4,588,604	91,489	29,430,921	4,852,663	90,125	31,732,121	4,864,472
ecc	24,150	13,451,827 a	3,120,351 a	23,889	13,546,159 a	3,258,595 a	23,504	13,931,409	3,269,986
ecv	90,985 a	93,071,869 a	16,732,701 a	89,511	93,765,006 a	16,482,315	90,919 a	101,746,341 a	17,874,955 a
elc	3,878,055	1,399,419,800	189,605,837	3,861,418	1,452,000,815	188,393,158	3,849,692	1,502,746,601	187,145,886
els	15,929 a	6,944,522 a	1,271,058 a	15,780	6,759,222 a	1,100,660	15,960	7,288,521	1,195,698
emc	4,059	3,834,001	2,299,864	4,130 a	4,260,307 a	1,406,682 a	4,225 a	4,597,730 a	1,533,157 a
feb	1,872 a	1,343,225 a	397,553 a	1,866 a	1,294,646 a	429,023 a	1,898 a	1,537,041 a	395,719 a
fmc	58,220	60,584,079	10,591,064	59,156	62,478,294	10,513,187	59,354 a	65,359,325 a	10,708,854 a
fum	50,005 e	NA	NA	45,542 e	NA	NA	44,771 e	NA	NA
ggb	72,388 a	21,561,432 a	1,402,330 a	73,129 a	22,376,970 a	1,440,342 a	71,140 a	19,651,624 a	2,052,409 a
lca	See ELCA	See ELCA	See ELCA	See ELCA	See ELCA	See ELCA	See ELCA	See ELCA	See ELCA
lms	1,953,248	777,467,488	131,684,905	1,945,077	789,821,559	130,761,788	1,944,905	817,412,113	129,525,358
mch	94,222 a	68,118,222	28,835,719	95,634	71,385,271	27,973,380	87,911 a	64,651,639	24,830,192
mca	22,533	10,150,953	1,208,372	22,223	9,675,502	1,191,131	21,448	9,753,010	1,182,778
nab	43,446	28,375,947	7,327,594	43,045	30,676,902	7,454,087	43,236	32,800,560	7,515,707
opc	12,580 a	12,466,266 a	3,025,824 a	12,924 a	13,158,089 a	3,039,676 a	13,970	14,393,880	3,120,454
pch	2,780,406	1,696,092,968	309,069,530	2,742,192	1,700,918,712	310,375,024	2,698,262	1,800,008,292	307,158,749
rca	190,322 a	147,181,320 a	28,457,900 a	188,551 a	159,715,941 a	26,009,853 a	185,242	153,107,408	27,906,830
sda	748,687	191,362,737	476,902,779	761,703	209,524,570	473,769,831	775,349	229,596,444	503,347,816
sbc	15,358,866	4,462,915,112	751,366,698	15,398,642	4,621,157,751	761,298,249	15,614,060	5,263,421,764	815,360,696
ucc	1,555,382	521,190,413	73,906,372	1,530,178	550,847,702	71,046,517	1,501,310	556,540,722	67,269,762
wel	316,183 a	127,858,970 a	26,426,128 a	315,871	137,187,582	24,587,988	315,302	142,851,919	23,998,935
Total	29,730,561	10,946,460,808	2,310,456,991	29,705,072	11,301,818,983	2,314,251,242	29,765,898	12,182,113,323	2,393,182,924

a Data obtained from denominational source.
e Inclusive membership used only in Chapter 5 analysis.
Note: Data in italics indicates a change from the previous edition in the series.

Appendix B-1: Church Member Giving, 1968-1996

	Data Year 1995			Data Year 1996		
	Full/Confirmed Members	Congregational Finances	Benevolences	Full/Confirmed Members	Congregational Finances	Benevolences
abc	726,452a	365,873,197a	57,052,333a	670,363a	351,362,401a	55,982,392a
alc	See ELCA	See ELCA	See ELCA	See ELCA	See ELCA	See ELCA
arp	33,513	23,399,372a	5,711,882a	34,117	24,452,824	5,871,337
bcc	18,529	16,032,149	5,480,828	18,424	16,892,154	4,748,871
ccd	601,237	357,895,652	42,887,958	586,131	370,210,746	42,877,144
cga	224,061	160,897,147	26,192,559	229,240	180,581,111	26,983,385
cgg	3,877	2,722,766	486,661	3,920	2,926,516	491,348
chb	143,121	60,242,418	22,599,214	NA	NA	NA
chn	598,946	396,698,137	93,440,095	608,008a	419,450,850a	95,358,352a
ccc	38,853a	24,250,819a	5,483,659a	38,788a	24,188,163a	5,369,693a
cpc	87,896	33,535,975	5,051,095	88,066	34,921,064	5,487,460
ecc	23,422	14,830,454	3,301,060	23,091	14,692,608	3,273,685
ecv	91,458	109,776,363a	17,565,085a	91,823a	115,693,329a	18,726,756a
elc	3,845,063	1,551,842,465	188,107,066	3,838,750	1,629,909,672	191,476,141
els	16,543	7,712,358a	1,084,136	16,511	8,136,195	1,104,996
emc	4,284a	5,321,079a	1,603,548a	4,201	5,361,912a	1,793,267a
feb	1,856a	1,412,281a	447,544a	1,751a	1,198,120a	507,656a
fmc	59,060	67,687,955	11,114,804	59,343a	70,262,626	11,651,462
fum	43,440 e	NA	NA	42,918 e	NA	NA
ggb	70,886a	24,385,956a	1,722,662a	70,562a	27,763,966a	1,832,909a
lca	See ELCA	See ELCA	See ELCA	See ELCA	See ELCA	See ELCA
lms	1,943,281	832,701,255	130,511,413	1,951,730	855,461,015	141,832,564
mch	90,139a	71,641,773	26,832,240	90,959	76,669,365	27,812,549
mca	21,409	10,996,031	1,167,513	21,140	11,798,536	1,237,349
nab	43,928	37,078,473	7,480,331	43,744a	37,172,560a	7,957,860a
opc	14,355	16,017,003	3,376,691	15,072a	17,883,915a	3,467,207a
pch	2,665,276	1,855,684,719	309,978,224	2,631,466	1,930,179,808	322,336,258
rca	183,255	164,250,624	29,995,068	182,342	159,247,507	31,271,007
sda	790,731	240,565,576	503,334,129	809,159	242,316,834	524,977,061
sbc	15,663,296	5,625,227,440f	858,635,435	15,691,249a	5,987,033,115	891,149,403a
ucc	1,472,213	578,042,965	67,806,448	1,452,565	615,727,028	69,013,791
wel	314,188a	150,853,785a	33,193,286a	314,379a	156,966,741a	44,370,503a
Total	29,791,128	12,807,576,187	2,461,642,967	29,586,894	13,388,460,681	2,538,962,406

aData obtained from denominational source.

eInclusive membership used only in Chapter 5 analysis.

f1995 Congregational Finances figure is an average of the Congregational Finances data for 1994 and 1996, based on information from the denomination.

Note: Data in italics indicates a change from the previous edition in the series.

Appendix B-2: Church Member Giving for 44 Denominations, 1995-1996

	Data Year 1995			Data Year 1996		
	Full/Confirmed Members	Congregational Finances	Benevolences	Full/Confirmed Members	Congregational Finances	Benevolences
Albanian Orthodox Diocese of America	1,984	167,500	15,600	1,995	164,600	7,300
Allegheny Wesleyan Methodist Connection (Original Allegheny Conference)	1,899	3,225,087	942,938	1,865	3,250,449	1,127,594
Baptist Missionary Association of America	231,191	52,609,191	10,198,727	232,069	53,752,512	10,858,764
Church of Lutheran Brethren of America	8,114	7,840,161 [a]	1,782,774 [a]	8,181	8,606,432	1,812,818
Church of the Lutheran Confession	6,474	3,276,827	698,962	6,657	3,685,658	673,511
Churches of God General Conference	31,745	16,822,826	3,637,695	31,558	17,136,919	3,646,977
The Episcopal Church	1,585,930 [a]	1,565,904,844	256,555,466	1,592,653	1,558,103,733	249,819,633 [a]
Evangelical Presbyterian Church	52,031 [a]	78,542,318 [a]	8,151,711 [a]	53,100	93,398,409 [a]	9,693,588 [a]
International Pentecostal Church of Christ	2,311	2,215,078	1,836,821	2,369	2,313,174	2,142,620
The Latvian Evangelical Lutheran Church in America	16,700 [a]	3,004,427	453,947	15,200	2,652,000	439,000 [a]
Missionary Church, Inc.	29,542	38,085,125	7,403,580	31,548	42,282,238 [a]	7,727,424 [a]
National Association of Free Will Baptists	213,716	44,222,933 [a]	8,777,067 [a]	210,305	57,244,171 [a]	9,687,919 [a]
Primitive Methodist Church in the U.S.A.	5,130	4,305,211	4,869,635 [a]	5,019	4,206,365	4,567,896
United Brethren in Christ	24,095	16,567,272	3,092,056	24,137	20,011,538	3,277,564
The United Methodist Church	8,538,808 [a]	2,825,152,360 [a]	743,206,974 [a]	8,496,047 [a]	2,984,250,917	760,441,306
The Wesleyan Church	109,150	126,917,905	29,232,828	111,099	135,664,782	25,945,862

[a]Data obtained from denominational source.

Appendix B-3.1: Church Member Giving for Eleven Denominations, 1921-1952, in Current Dollars

Year	Total Contributions	Members	Per Capita Giving
1921	$281,173,263	17,459,611	$16.10
1922	345,995,802	18,257,426	18.95
1923	415,556,876	18,866,775	22.03
1924	443,187,826	19,245,220	23.03
1925	412,658,363	19,474,863	21.19
1926	368,529,223	17,054,404	21.61
1927	459,527,624	20,266,709	22.67
1928	429,947,883	20,910,584	20.56
1929	445,327,233	20,612,910	21.60
1930	419,697,819	20,796,745	20.18
1931	367,158,877	21,508,745	17.07
1932	309,409,873	21,757,411	14.22
1933	260,366,681	21,792,663	11.95
1934	260,681,472	22,105,624	11.79
1935	267,596,925	22,204,355	12.05
1936	279,835,526	21,746,023	12.87
1937	297,134,313	21,906,456	13.56
1938	307,217,666	22,330,090	13.76
1939	302,300,476	23,084,048	13.10
1940	311,362,429	23,671,660	13.15
1941	336,732,622	23,120,929	14.56
1942	358,419,893	23,556,204	15.22
1943	400,742,492	24,679,784	16.24
1944	461,500,396	25,217,319	18.30
1945	551,404,448	25,898,642	21.29
1946	608,165,179	26,158,559	23.25
1947	684,393,895	27,082,905	25.27
1948	775,360,993	27,036,992	28.68
1949	875,069,944	27,611,824	31.69
1950	934,723,015	28,176,095	33.17
1951	1,033,391,527	28,974,314	35.67
1952	1,121,802,639	29,304,909	38.28

Appendix B-3.2: Church Member Giving for Eleven Denominations, 1953-1967

	Data Year 1953		Data Year 1954		Data Year 1955	
	Total Contributions	Per Capita Total Contributions	Total Contributions	Per Capita Total Contributions	Total Contributions	Per Capita Total Contributions
American Baptist (Northern)	$66,557,447 [a]	$44.50 [b]	$65,354,184	$43.17	$67,538,753 [d]	$44.19
Christian Ch (Disciples of Christ)	$60,065,545 [c]	$32.50 [b]	$65,925,164	$34.77	$68,611,162 [d]	$35.96
Church of the Brethren	$7,458,584	$43.78	$7,812,806	$45.88	$9,130,616	$53.00
The Episcopal Church	$84,209,027	$49.02	$92,079,668	$51.84	$97,541,567 [d]	$50.94 [b]
Evangelical Lutheran Church in Am.						
The American Lutheran Church						
American Lutheran Church	$30,881,256	$55.24	$34,202,987	$58.83	$40,411,856	$67.03
The Evangelical Lutheran Church	$30,313,907	$48.70	$33,312,926	$51.64	$37,070,341	$55.29
United Evangelical Lutheran Ch.	$1,953,163	$55.85	$2,268,200	$50.25	$2,635,469	$69.84
Lutheran Free Church	Not Reported: YACC 1955, p. 264		$2,101,026	$44.51	$2,708,747	$55.76
Evan. Lutheran Churches,Assn of	Not Reported: YACC 1955, p. 264		Not Reported: YACC 1956, p. 276		Not Reported: YACC 1957, p. 284	
Lutheran Church in America						
United Lutheran Church	$67,721,548	$45.68	$76,304,344	$50.25	$83,170,787	$53.46
General Council Evang Luth Ch						
General Synod of Evan Luth Ch						
United Syn Evang Luth South						
American Evangelical Luth. Ch	Not Reported: YACC 1955, p. 264		Not Reported: YACC 1956, p. 276		Not Reported: YACC 1957, p. 284	
Augustana Lutheran Church	$18,733,019	$53.98	$22,203,098	$62.14	$22,090,350	$60.12
Finnish Luth. Ch (Suomi Synod)	$744,971	$32.12	$674,554	$29.47	$1,059,682	$43.75
Moravian Church in Am. No. Prov.	$1,235,534	$53.26	$1,461,658	$59.51	$1,241,008	$49.15
Presbyterian Church (U.S.A.)						
United Presbyterian Ch in U.S.A.						
Presbyterian Ch in the U.S.A.	$141,057,179	$56.49	$158,110,613	$61.47	$180,472,698	$68.09
United Presbyterian Ch in N.A.	$13,204,897	$57.73	$14,797,353	$62.37	$16,019,616	$65.39
Presbyterian Church in the U.S.	$56,001,996	$73.99	$59,222,983	$75.54	$66,033,260	$81.43
Reformed Church in America	$13,671,897	$68.57	$14,740,275	$71.87	$17,459,572	$84.05
Southern Baptist Convention	$278,851,129	$39.84	$305,573,654	$42.17	$334,836,283	$44.54
United Church of Christ						
Congregational Christian	$64,061,866	$49.91	$71,786,834	$54.76	$80,519,810	$60.00
Congregational						
Evangelical and Reformed	$31,025,133	$41.24	$36,261,267	$46.83	$41,363,406	$52.74
Evangelical Synod of N.A./German						
Reformed Church in the U.S.						
The United Methodist Church						
The Evangelical United Brethren	$36,331,994	$50.21	$36,609,598	$50.43	$41,199,631	$56.01
The Methodist Church	$314,521,214	$34.37	$345,416,448	$37.53	$389,490,613	$41.82
Methodist Episcopal Church						
Methodist Episcopal Ch South						
Methodist Protestant Church						
Total	$1,318,601,306		$1,446,219,640		$1,600,655,226	

[a] In data year 1953, $805,135 has been subtracted from the 1955 Yearbook of American Churches (Edition for 1956) entry. See 1956 Yearbook of American Churches (Edition for 1957), p. 276, n.1.

[b] To obtain comparable membership figures in order to calculate giving as a percentage of income based on the revised Total Contributions data, the Total Contributions figure as published in the Yearbook was divided by the published per capita figure yielding a membership figure. The revised Total Contributions figure was then divided by the total calculated membership to obtain the revised per capita figure included in the above table.

[c] In data year 1953, $5,508,883 has been added to the 1955 Yearbook of American Churches (Edition for 1956) entry. See 1956 Yearbook of American Churches (Edition for 1957), p. 276, n. 4.

[d] Total Contributions averaged from available data as follows: The Episcopal Church, 1954 and 1956 data; American Baptist Churches, 1954 and 1957 data; Christian Church (Disiples of Christ), 1954 and 1956 data.

Appendix B-3.2: Church Member Giving for Eleven Denominations, 1953-1967 (continued)

	Data Year 1956		Data Year 1957		Data Year 1958	
	Total Contributions	Per Capita Total Contributions	Total Contributions	Per Capita Total Contributions	Total Contributions	Per Capita Total Contributions
American Baptist (Northern)	$69,723,321 d	$45.21	$71,907,890	$46.23	$70,405,404	$45.03
Christian Ch (Disciples of Christ)	$71,397,159	$37.14	$73,737,955	$37.94	$79,127,458	$41.17
Church of the Brethren	$10,936,285	$63.15	$11,293,388	$64.43	$12,288,049	$70.03
The Episcopal Church	$103,003,465	$52.79	$111,660,728	$53.48	$120,687,177	$58.33
Evangelical Lutheran Church in Am.						
The American Lutheran Church						
American Lutheran Church	$45,316,809	$72.35	$44,518,194	$68.80	$47,216,896	$70.89
The Evangelical Lutheran Church	$39,096,038	$56.47	$44,212,046	$61.95	$45,366,512	$61.74
United Evangelical Lutheran Ch.	$2,843,527	$73.57	$2,641,201	$65.46	$3,256,050	$77.38
Lutheran Free Church	$2,652,307	$53.14	$3,379,882	$64.70	$3,519,017	$66.31
Evan. Lutheran Churches,Assn of	Not Reported: YACC 1958, p. 292		Not Reported: YACC 1959, p. 277		Not Reported: YACC 1960, p. 276	
Lutheran Church in America						
United Lutheran Church	$93,321,223	$58.46	$100,943,860	$61.89	$110,179,054	$66.45
General Council Evang Luth Ch						
General Synod of Evan Luth Ch						
United Syn Evang Luth South						
American Evangelical Luth. Ch	Not Comparable (YACC 1958, p. 292)		$935,319	$59.45	$1,167,503	$72.98
Augustana Lutheran Church	$24,893,792	$66.15	$28,180,152	$72.09	$29,163,771	$73.17
Finnish Luth. Ch (Suomi Synod)	$1,308,026	$51.56	$1,524,299	$58.11	$1,533,058	$61.94
Moravian Church in Am. No. Prov.	$1,740,961	$67.53	$1,776,703	$67.77	$1,816,281	$68.14
Presbyterian Church (U.S.A.)						
United Presbyterian Ch in U.S.A.					$243,000,572	$78.29
Presbyterian Ch in the U.S.A.	$204,208,085	$75.02	$214,253,598	$77.06		
United Presbyterian Ch in N.A.	$18,424,936	$73.30	$19,117,837	$74.24		
Presbyterian Church in the U.S.	$73,477,555	$88.56	$78,426,424	$92.03	$82,760,291	$95.18
Reformed Church in America	$18,718,008	$88.56	$19,658,604	$91.10	$21,550,017	$98.24
Southern Baptist Convention	$372,136,675	$48.17	$397,540,347	$49.99	$419,619,438	$51.04
United Church of Christ						
Congregational Christian	$89,914,505	$65.18	$90,333,453	$64.87	$97,480,446	$69.55
Congregational						
Evangelical and Reformed	$51,519,531	$64.88	$55,718,141	$69.56	$63,419,468	$78.56
Evangelical Synod of N.A./German						
Reformed Church in the U.S.						
The United Methodist Church						
The Evangelical United Brethren	$44,727,060	$60.57	$45,738,332 d	$61.75	$46,749,605 d	$62.93
The Methodist Church	$413,893,955	$43.82	$462,826,269 d	$48.31	$511,758,582	$52.80
Methodist Episcopal Church						
Methodist Episcopal Ch South						
Methodist Protestant Church						
Total	$1,753,253,223		$1,880,324,622		$2,012,064,649	

d Total Contributions averaged from available data as follows: 1956 American Baptist Churches, 1954 and 1957 data; 1957 and 1958 Evangelical United Brethren, 1956 and 1960 data; 1957 The Methodist Church, 1956 and 1958 data.

Appendix B-3.2: Church Member Giving for Eleven Denominations, 1953-1967 (continued)

	Data Year 1959		Data Year 1960		Data Year 1961	
	Total Contributions	Per Capita Total Contributions	Total Contributions	Per Capita Total Contributions	Total Contributions	Per Capita Total Contributions
American Baptist (Northern)	$74,877,669	$48.52	$73,106,232	$48.06	$104,887,025	$68.96
Christian Ch (Disciples of Christ)	$84,375,152 d	$51.22	$86,834,944	$63.26	$89,730,589	$65.31
Church of the Brethren	$12,143,983	$65.27	$12,644,194	$68.33	$13,653,155	$73.33
The Episcopal Church	$130,279,752	$61.36	$140,625,284	$64.51	$154,458,809	$68.30
Evangelical Lutheran Church in America						
The American Lutheran Church	$50,163,078	$73.52	$51,898,875	$74.49	$113,645,260	$73.28
American Lutheran Church	$49,488,063	$65.56	$51,297,348	$66.85		
The Evangelical Lutheran Church	Not Reported: YACC 1961, p. 273		Not Reported: YACC 1963, p. 273			
United Evangelical Lutheran Church	$3,354,270	$61.20	$3,618,418	$63.98	$4,316,925	$73.46
Lutheran Free Church	Not Reported: YACC 1961, p. 273		Not Reported: YACC 1963, p. 273			
Evangelical Lutheran Churches,Assn of						
Lutheran Church in America						
United Lutheran Church	$114,458,260	$68.29	$119,447,895	$70.86	$128,850,845	$76.18
General Council Evang Luth Ch						
General Synod of Evan Luth Ch						
United Syn Evang Luth South						
American Evangelical Lutheran Ch	$1,033,907	$63.83	$1,371,600	$83.63	$1,209,752	$74.89
Augustana Lutheran Church	$31,279,335	$76.97	$33,478,865	$80.88	$37,863,105	$89.37
Finnish Lutheran Ch (Suomi Synod)	$1,685,342	$68.61	$1,860,481	$76.32	$1,744,550	$70.60
Moravian Church in America, No. Prov.	$2,398,565	$89.28	$2,252,536	$82.95	$2,489,930	$90.84
Presbyterian Church (U.S.A.)	$259,679,057	$82.30	$270,233,943	$84.31	$285,380,476	$87.90
United Presbyterian Ch in U.S.A.						
Presbyterian Ch in the U.S.A.						
United Presbyterian Ch in N.A.						
Presbyterian Church in the U.S.	$88,404,631	$99.42	$91,582,428	$101.44	$96,637,354	$105.33
Reformed Church in America	$22,970,935	$103.23	$23,615,749	$104.53	$25,045,773	$108.80
Southern Baptist Convention	$453,338,720	$53.88	$480,608,972	$55.68	$501,301,714	$50.24
United Church of Christ	$100,938,267	$71.12	$104,862,037	$73.20	$105,871,158	$73.72
Congregational Christian						
Congregational						
Evangelical and Reformed	$65,541,874	$80.92	$62,346,084	$76.58	$65,704,662	$80.33
Evangelical Synod of N.A./German						
Reformed Church in the U.S.						
The United Methodist Church						
The Evangelical United Brethren	$47,760,877 e	$64.10	$48,772,149	$65.28	$50,818,912	$68.12
The Methodist Church	$532,854,842 e	$53.97	$553,951,102	$55.14	$581,504,618	$57.27
Methodist Episcopal Church						
Methodist Episcopal Ch South						
Methodist Protestant Church						
Total	$2,127,026,579		$2,214,409,136		$2,365,114,612	

d The 1961 YACC, pa. 273 indicates that this data is not comparable.
e The Evangelical United Brethren and The Methodist Church data is calculated from available data.

Appendix B-3.2: Church member Giving for Eleven Denominations, 1953-1967 (continued)

	Data Year 1962		Data Year 1963		Data Year 1964	
	Total Contributions	Per Capita Total Contributions	Total Contributions	Per Capita Total Contributions	Total Contributions	Per Capita Total Contributions
American Baptist (Northern)	$105,667,332	$68.42	$99,001,651	$68.34	$104,699,557	$69.99
Christian Ch (Disciples of Christ)	$91,889,457	$67.20	$96,607,038	$75.81	$102,102,840	$86.44
Church of the Brethren	$14,594,572	$77.88	$14,574,688	$72.06	$15,221,162	$76.08
The Episcopal Church	$155,971,264	$69.80	$171,125,464	$76.20	$175,374,777	$76.66
Evangelical Lutheran Church in America						
The American Lutheran Church	$114,912,112	$72.47	$136,202,292	$81.11	$143,687,165	$83.83
American Lutheran Church						
The Evangelical Lutheran Church						
United Evangelical Luth. Church						
Lutheran Free Church	$4,765,138	$78.68				
Evangelical Luth. Churches, Assn of						
Lutheran Church in America	$185,166,857	$84.98	$157,423,391	$71.45	$170,012,096	$76.35
United Lutheran Church						
General Council Evang Luth Ch						
General Synod of Evan Luth Ch						
United Syn Evang Luth South						
American Evangelical Luth. Ch						
Augustana Lutheran Church						
Finnish Luth. Ch (Suomi Synod)						
Moravian Church in Am., No. Prov.	$2,512,133	$91.92	$2,472,273	$89.29	$2,868,694	$103.54
Presbyterian Church (U.S.A.)						
United Presbyterian Ch in U.S.A.	$288,496,652	$88.08	$297,582,313	$90.46	$304,833,435	$92.29
Presbyterian Ch in the U.S.A.						
United Presbyterian Ch in N.A.						
Presbyterian Church in the U.S.	$99,262,431	$106.96	$102,625,764	$109.46	$108,269,579	$114.61
Reformed Church in America	$25,579,443	$110.16	$26,918,484	$117.58	$29,174,103	$126.44
Southern Baptist Convention	$540,811,457	$53.06	$556,042,694	$53.49	$591,587,981	$55.80
United Church of Christ	$164,858,968	$72.83	$162,379,019	$73.12	$169,208,042	$75.94
Congregational Christian						
Congregational						
Evangelical and Reformed						
Evangelical Synod of N.A./German Reformed Church in the U.S.						
The United Methodist Church						
The Evangelical United Brethren	$54,567,962	$72.91	$49,921,568	$67.37	$56,552,783	$76.34
The Methodist Church	$599,081,561	$58.53	$613,547,721	$59.60	$608,841,881	$59.09
Methodist Episcopal Church						
Methodist Episcopal Ch South						
Methodist Protestant Church						
Total	$2,448,137,339		$2,486,424,360		$2,582,434,095	

NOTE: Data for the years 1965 through 1967 was not available in a form that could be readily analyzed for the present purposes, and therefore data for 1965-1967 was estimated as described in the introductory comments to Appendix B. See Appendix B-1 for 1968-1991 data except for The Episcopal Church and The United Methodist Church, available data for which is presented in the continuation of Appendix B-3 in the table immediately following.

Appendix B-3.3: Church Member Giving for Eleven Denominations, The Episcopal Church and The United Methodist Church, 1968-1996

The Episcopal Church		
Data Year	Total Contributions	Full/Confirmed Membership
1968	$194,057,895	2,260,950
1969	$198,728,675	2,238,538
1970	$248,702,969	2,208,773
1971	$257,523,469	2,143,557
1972	$270,245,645	2,099,896
1973	$287,937,285 c	2,084,845 c
1974	$305,628,925	2,069,793
1975	$352,243,222	2,051,964
1976	$375,942,065	2,021,057
1977	$401,814,395	2,114,638
1978	$430,116,564	1,975,234
1979	$484,211,412	1,962,062
1980	$507,315,457	1,933,487
1981	$697,816,298	1,930,690
1982	$778,184,068	1,922,205
1983	$876,844,252	1,906,618
1984	$939,796,743	1,896,056
1985	$1,043,117,983	1,881,250
1986	$1,134,455,479	1,756,120
1987	$1,181,378,441	1,741,036
1988	$1,209,378,098	1,725,581
1989	$1,309,243,747	1,714,122
1990	$1,377,794,610	1,698,240
1991	$1,433,467,803	1,615,505
1992	$1,582,457,015 d	1,614,081 d
1993	$1,613,697,551	1,570,444
1994	$1,696,658,859 d	1,577,996 d
1995	$1,822,460,310	1,585,930
1996	$1,807,923,366	1,592,653

The United Methodist Church		
Data Year	Total Contributions	Full/Confirmed Membership
1968	$763,000,434 a	10,849,375 b
1969	$800,425,000	10,671,774
1970	$819,945,000	10,509,198
1971	$843,103,000	10,334,521
1972	$885,708,000	10,192,265
1973	$935,723,000	10,063,046
1974	$1,009,760,804	9,957,710
1975	$1,081,080,372	9,861,028
1976	$1,162,828,991	9,785,534
1977	$1,264,191,548	9,731,779
1978	$1,364,460,266	9,653,711
1979	$1,483,481,986	9,584,771
1980	$1,632,204,336	9,519,407
1981	$1,794,706,741	9,457,012
1982	$1,931,796,533	9,405,164
1983	$2,049,437,917	9,291,936
1984	$2,211,306,198	9,266,853
1985	$2,333,928,274	9,192,172
1986	$2,460,079,431	9,124,575
1987	$2,573,748,234	9,055,145
1988	$2,697,918,285	8,979,139
1989	$2,845,998,177	8,904,824
1990	$2,967,535,538	8,853,455
1991	$3,099,522,282	8,789,101
1992	$3,202,700,721 d	8,726,951 d
1993	$3,303,255,279	8,646,595
1994	$3,430,351,778	8,584,125
1995	$3,568,359,334 d	8,538,808 d
1996	$3,744,692,223	8,496,047 d

aThe Evangelical United Brethren Data Not Reported: YACC 1970, p. 198-200. This figure is the sum of The Methodist Church in 1968, and the Evangelical United Brethren data for 1967.
bThis membership figure is an average of the sum of 1967 membership for The Methodist Church and the Evangelical United Brethren and 1969 data for The United Methodist Church.
cThe Episcopal Church did not report financial data in the 1970 YACC (pp. 198-200) or the 1975 YACC (p. 236). The 1968 dollar figure is prorated based on 1964 and 1969 data for The Episcopal Church. The 1973 dollar figure is an average of 1972 and 1974 data for The Episcopal Church.
dData obtained directly from denominational source.
Note: Data in italics indicates a change from the previous edition in the series.

Appendix B-4: Trends in Giving and Membership

Appendix B-4.1: Membership for Seven Denominations, 1968-1996

Year	American Baptist Churches (Total Memb)	Assemblies of God	Baptist General Conference	Christian and Missionary Alliance	Church of God (Cleveland, TN)	Roman Catholic Church	Salvation Army
1968	1,583,560	610,946	100,000	71,656	243,532	47,468,333	329,515
1969	1,528,019	626,660	101,226	70,573	257,995	47,872,089	331,711
1970	1,472,478	625,027	103,955	71,708	272,276	48,214,729	326,934
1971	1,562,636	645,891	108,474	73,547	287,099	48,390,990	335,684
1972	1,484,393	679,813	111,364	77,991	297,103	48,460,427	358,626
1973	1,502,759	700,071	109,033	77,606	313,332	48,465,438	361,571
1974	1,579,029	751,818	111,093	80,412	328,892	48,701,835	366,471
1975	1,603,033	785,348	115,340	83,628	343,249	48,881,872	384,817
1976	1,593,574	898,711	117,973	83,978	365,124	49,325,752	380,618
1977	1,584,517	939,312	120,222	88,763	377,765	49,836,176	396,238
1978	1,589,610	932,365	131,000	88,903	392,551	49,602,035	414,035
1979	1,600,521	958,418	126,800	96,324	441,385	49,812,178	414,659
1980	1,607,541	1,064,490	133,385	106,050	435,012	50,449,842	417,359
1981	1,621,795	1,103,134	127,662	109,558	456,797	51,207,579	414,999
1982	1,637,099	1,119,686	129,928	112,745	463,992	52,088,774	419,475
1983	1,620,153	1,153,935	131,594	117,501	493,904	52,392,934	428,046
1984	1,559,683	1,189,143	131,162	120,250	505,775	52,286,043	420,971
1985	1,576,483	1,235,403	130,193	123,602	521,061	52,654,908	427,825
1986	1,568,778	1,258,724	132,546	130,116	536,346	52,893,217	432,893
1987	1,561,656	1,275,146	136,688	131,354	551,632	53,496,862	434,002
1988	1,548,573	1,275,148	134,396	133,575	556,917	54,918,949	433,448
1989	1,535,971	1,266,982	135,125	134,336	582,203	57,019,948	445,566
1990	1,527,840	1,298,121	133,742	138,071	620,393	58,568,015	445,991
1991	1,534,078	1,324,800	134,717	141,077	646,201	58,267,424	446,403
1992	1,538,710	1,337,321	134,658	142,346	672,008	59,220,723	450,028
1993	1,516,505	1,340,400	134,814	147,367	700,517	59,858,042	450,312
1994	1,507,934	1,354,337	135,128	147,560	722,541	60,190,605	443,246
1995	1,517,400	1,377,320	135,008	147,955	753,230	60,280,454	453,150
1996	1,503,267	1,407,941	136,120	143,157	773,483	61,207,914	462,744

Note regarding American Baptist Churches in the U.S.A. Total Membership data: Total Membership is used for the American Baptist Churches in the U.S.A. for analyses that consider membership as a percentage of U.S. population. The ABC denominational ofice is the source for this data in the years 1968 and from 1986 through 1992. The year 1969 is an average of the years 1968 and 1970. The year 1978 Total Membership data figure is a *YACC* adjusted figure.

Appendix C: Income, Deflators, and U.S. Population

Appendix C.1 presents U.S. Per Capita Disposable Personal Income for 1921 through 1996. The Implicit Price Index for Gross National Product is provided for 1921 through 1996. The series keyed to 1992 dollars provided deflators only from 1929 through 1996. Therefore, the 1921 through 1928 data was converted to inflation-adjusted 1958 dollars using the series keyed to 1958=100, and the inflation-adjusted 1958 dollar values were then converted to inflation-adjusted 1992 dollars using the series keyed to 1992 dollars. Appendix C.2 presents U.S. population for 1921 through 1996.

SOURCES
Income 1921-1928, Deflator 1921-1928, and U.S. Population, 1921-1928
Historical Statistics of the United States: Colonial Times to 1970 Bicentennial Edition, Part 1 (Washington, DC: Bureau of the Census, 1975):
   1921-28 Per Capita Disposable Personal Income: Series F 9, p. 224 (F 6-9).
   1921-28 Implicit Price Index GNP (1958=100): Series F 9, p. 224 (F 6-9).
   1921-28 U.S. population: Series A-7, p. 8 (A6-8).
Income 1929-1981

   Per Capita Disposable Personal Income in Current Dollars: U.S. Department of Commerce, Bureau of Economic Analysis, National Income and Product Accounts of the United States, 1929-94, Volume 2. Washington, DC: U.S. Government Printing Office, 1998, Table 8.3, p. 306.

Income 1982-94

   Per Capita Disposable Personal Income in Current Dollars: U.S. Department of Commerce, Bureau of Economic Analysis, *Survey of Current Business*, August 1998, Table 2.1, p. 128.

Income 1995-96

   Per Capita Disposable Personal Income in Current Dollars: U.S. Department of Commerce, Bureau of Economic Analysis, *Survey of Current Business*, August 1998, Table 8.2, p. 109.
Deflator in 1992 Dollars, 1929-1996

   Gross National Product: Implicit Price Deflators for Gross National Product: U.S. Bureau of Economic Analysis, *Survey of Current Business*, August 1998, Table 3, p. 159.
U.S. Population 1929-1958

   U.S. Population: U.S. Department of Commerce, Bureau of Economic Analysis, National Income and Product Accounts of the United States: Vol. 1, 1929-58, February 1993, Table 8.2, p. 190.

U.S. Population 1959-88

   U.S. Population: U.S. Department of Commerce, Bureau of Economic Analysis, National Income and Product Accounts of the United States: Vol. 2, 1959-88, September 1992, Table 8.2, p. 330.

U.S. Population 1989-96

   U.S. Population: U.S. Department of Commerce, Bureau of Economic Analysis, *Survey of Current Business*
   1989: December 1991, p. 16.
   1990-93: July 1994, p. 111.
   1994: July 1996, p. 27.
   1995: May 1997, p. D-25.
   1996: July 1998, Table 8.3, p. D-25.

Appendix C.1: Per Capita Disposable Personal Income and Deflators, 1921-1996

Year	Current $s Per Capita Disposable Personal Income	Implicit Price Deflator GNP [1958= 100]	Implicit Price Deflator GNP [1992= 100]
1921	$555	54.5	
1922	$548	50.1	
1923	$623	51.3	
1924	$626	51.2	
1925	$630	51.9	
1926	$659	51.1	
1927	$650	50.0	
1928	$643	50.8	
1929	$680		13.12
1930	$602		12.65
1931	$515		11.34
1932	$390		10.02
1933	$363		9.74
1934	$414		10.28
1935	$461		10.47
1936	$520		10.59
1937	$554		11.04
1938	$506		10.72
1939	$539		10.61
1940	$575		10.76
1941	$697		11.50
1942	$872		12.35
1943	$982		13.02
1944	$1,062		13.36
1945	$1,077		13.72
1946	$1,136		15.38
1947	$1,185		17.10
1948	$1,297		18.10
1949	$1,272		18.10
1950	$1,382		18.29
1951	$1,492		19.60
1952	$1,545		19.94
1953	$1,617		20.19
1954	$1,625		20.41
1955	$1,710		20.75
1956	$1,794		21.47
1957	$1,859		22.18
1958	$1,892		22.72
1959	$1,975		22.96

Year	Current $s Per Capita Disposable Personal Income	Implicit Price Deflator GNP [1992= 100]
1960	$2,013	23.28
1961	$2,066	23.55
1962	$2,156	23.85
1963	$2,229	24.13
1964	$2,389	24.49
1965	$2,546	24.97
1966	$2,720	25.68
1967	$2,882	26.50
1968	$3,101	27.66
1969	$3,302	28.96
1970	$3,550	30.50
1971	$3,811	32.08
1972	$4,082	33.44
1973	$4,562	35.32
1974	$4,941	38.49
1975	$5,383	42.11
1976	$5,856	44.58
1977	$6,383	47.46
1978	$7,123	50.92
1979	$7,888	55.26
1980	$8,697	60.36
1981	$9,601	66.05
1982	$10,132	70.21
1983	$10,776	73.20
1984	$11,912	75.97
1985	$12,592	78.57
1986	$13,211	80.62
1987	$13,851	83.09
1988	$14,881	86.12
1989	$15,771	89.75
1990	$16,689	93.63
1991	$17,179	97.33
1992	$18,029	100.00
1993	$18,558	102.63
1994	$19,251	105.08
1995	$20,050	107.49
1996	$20,840	109.50

Appendix C.2: U.S. Population, 1921-1996

Year	U.S. Population	Year	U.S. Population
1921	108,538,000	1960	180,760,000
1922	110,049,000	1961	183,742,000
1923	111,947,000	1962	186,590,000
1924	114,109,000	1963	189,300,000
1925	115,829,000	1964	191,927,000
1926	117,397,000	1965	194,347,000
1927	119,035,000	1966	196,599,000
1928	120,509,000	1967	198,752,000
1929	121,878,000	1968	200,745,000
1930	123,188,000	1969	202,736,000
1931	124,149,000	1970	205,089,000
1932	124,949,000	1971	207,692,000
1933	125,690,000	1972	209,924,000
1934	126,485,000	1973	211,939,000
1935	127,362,000	1974	213,898,000
1936	128,181,000	1975	215,981,000
1937	128,961,000	1976	218,086,000
1938	129,969,000	1977	220,289,000
1939	131,028,000	1978	222,629,000
1940	132,122,000	1979	225,106,000
1941	133,402,000	1980	227,715,000
1942	134,860,000	1981	229,989,000
1943	136,739,000	1982	232,201,000
1944	138,397,000	1983	234,326,000
1945	139,928,000	1984	236,393,000
1946	141,389,000	1985	238,510,000
1947	144,126,000	1986	240,691,000
1948	146,631,000	1987	242,860,000
1949	149,188,000	1988	245,093,000
1950	151,684,000	1989	247,405,000
1951	154,287,000	1990	249,951,000
1952	156,954,000	1991	252,688,000
1953	159,565,000	1992	255,484,000
1954	162,391,000	1993	258,290,000
1955	165,275,000	1994	260,681,000
1956	168,221,000	1995	263,090,000
1957	171,274,000	1996	265,579,000
1958	174,141,000		
1959	177,073,000		